# The Official Sherlock Holmes Trivia Book

by

## Richard T. Ryan

QUINLAN PRESS

Boston

*Published by:*
Quinlan Press
131 Beverly Street
Boston, MA 02114

ISBN 0-933341-99-7
LC 87-43037

Cover design by Chris Bergan

Printed in the United States of America, 1987

## Dedication

This book is dedicated to the memory of my father, Edward John Ryan, "whom I shall ever regard as the best and the wisest man whom I have ever known."

In addition to being a devoted Sherlockian and a member of the Priory Scholars Scion of the Baker Street Irregular, *Richard T. Ryan* teaches English in a secondary school and works for a local New York newspaper, *The Staten Island Register*, as a theater critic. He holds a master's degree from the University of Notre Dame, and has had articles appear in such publications as *Genesis, Marine Corps Gazette, Commonweal,* and *Educational Studies,* among others. Ryan recently had his first full-length play, *Deadly Relations,* produced off-Broadway.

## Acknowledgments

While Sherlock Holmes quite often allowed Inspector Lestrade and the other members of Scotland Yard to take full credit for what he had accomplished, I should be as criminal as Moriarty if I failed to mention all those who have either encouraged or endured me during the composition of this book.

My biggest debt is to my wife, Grace, whose ceaseless encouragement, careful proofreading, and unflagging patience have seen this project grow from a vague idea to the book you have before you.

In addition to the rest of my family, I am also indebted to a number of my friends for any number of diverse reasons. Whether they have loaned me books and videotapes, made suggestions, or simply allowed me to pick their brains, I am beholding to Lou Giletta, Ed Burke, Chris Steinbrunner, John Gigante, Leonard Valenta, Bob Edelman, Mark Gosser of *TV Guide*, Sally Millwood of Grenada Television, and last, but certainly not least, Lou Wein.

Finally, I would like to thank my editor Sandy Bielawa for all her enthusiasm and patience, Lorrie Piatczyc, Kevin Stevens and all the rest of the staff at Quinlan Press.

# Contents

# Introduction

Sherlock Holmes would readily admit that his methods were "founded upon the observation of trifles," for "the gravest issues may depend upon the smallest things." And since "to a great mind nothing is little," and "all knowledge comes useful to a detective," this book has been assembled in the true spirit of Holmes himself to offer his devoted followers "some pretty little problems."

Readers of the Holmesian canon have often tried to emulate the Master and to incorporate his methods into their lives. This book will tell you if you have observed as Sherlock would have and whether you possess his "extraordinary gift for minutiae."

You should only take these quizzes if upon seeing this book you exclaimed, "The game is afoot!"

The questions in each chapter might be looked upon as "clues." Taken as a whole this book will indicate if, like the Master, you possess a wide range "of exact knowledge." Each "clue" has been assigned a point value ranging from one to five points. There are a few ten-pointers as well.

The tests, if you will, are based on the honor system, and guessing is permitted. At the conclusion of each chapter you simply total up the points you have accumulated from the various clues and see where you fit on the rating scale.

A score of 81 points or better in each chapter will qualify you as an "Official Surrogate Sherlock," while a total of 20 points or less indicates that "The Game Is *Still* Afoot!" It is more likely that your score will fall somewhere in between. Below is the complete rating system:

| | |
|---|---|
| 81-100 | Official Surrogate Sherlock |
| 61-80 | A Match for Moriarty |
| 41-60 | A Baker Street Irregular |
| 21-40 | A Scotland Yard Inspector |
| 0-20 | The Game Is *Still* Afoot! |

I hope you will find that you too possess "a strangely retentive memory for trifles," as well as "a vast store of out-of-the-way knowledge." Because after all, guessing "*is* a shocking habit—destructive to the logical faculty."

Richard T. Ryan

# Chapter 1
# The Very Worst Tenant
# in London

1. Before taking up residence at the now-famous 221B Baker Street, where was Holmes living?

2. Which three sports did Holmes enjoy in college?

3. Always a bit of a recluse, Holmes once told Watson that he had but a single friend during his college years. What was that individual's name?

4. Partial to all types of smoking, Holmes nevertheless seems to have preferred a pipe. Which was Holmes's favorite pipe?

5. What type of pipe tobacco did the Master prefer?

## The Very Worst Tenant—Questions

6.  Which of his pipes did Sherlock favor when he was in a "disputatious mood"?

7.  Where did the rather eccentric Holmes keep his tobacco?

8.  When he shunned his pipe, Holmes would often partake of cigars. Where would a visitor look to find Holmes's cache of cigars?

9.  Physically imposing, how tall did Holmes claim to be?

10. Aside from his physical stature, Holmes's most striking feature may have been his piercing eyes. What color were they?

11. Which did Sherlock tell Watson was "the first [case] in which I was ever engaged"?

12. For relaxation Sherlock often turned to music; when he wasn't listening to it, he was often playing it. What type of violin did the Master own?

13. From whom did Holmes acquire his instrument, and how much did he pay for it?

14. What was the name of the Master's grandmother?

15. Only one member of Sherlock's immediate family ever figures in the canon. What was the Christian name of Sherlock's sibling?

16. In describing himself, Holmes said that he was what kind of detective?

17. Although he was proficient in the use of many weapons, Watson tells us that Holmes had a favorite. What was the Master's preferred weapon?

18. We know that only two portraits adorned the walls of Baker Street. Whose visages gazed down on Holmes and Watson daily?

19. Which drug did Holmes take in a seven-percent solution during prolonged periods of inactivity?

20. One of Holmes more trying peculiarities was his tendency to engage in pistol practice—indoors! What initials had Holmes shot into the Baker Street walls?

21. Although he could most often be found at Baker Street, we are told that Sherlock kept a number of "refuges in different parts of London." How many of these sanctuaries did he maintain?

22. Holmes left his unanswered correspondence in a rather strange location which must have caused Mrs. Hudson a bit of consternation. Where did Holmes leave those letters he meant to answer?

23. Normally reticent, Holmes nevertheless wrote up two of his own cases. Which ones were they?

24. Many cases serve as testimony to Holmes's ability as an actor; however, only three of the parts played by Holmes in disguise were even given names. What were they?

25. Although Holmes took a deserved pride in his many successes, he was not so vain as to ignore his defeats. How many times did Sherlock admit to being beaten?

26. Despite the fact that Holmes was a prolific writer and authored many monographs upon a variety of subjects, we only know the titles of three of his compositions. What are those titles?

27. Sherlock cursed or swore in many stories, but only once are we told what he actually said. What were Holmes's exact words, and which case prompted such an untoward remark?

28. How many times did that motley crew of street Arabs which make up the Baker Street Irregulars ascend to Holmes's rooms *en masse*?

29. Who was the leader of the Baker Street Irregulars?

30. After a rather extensive career, Holmes retired to raise bees. Exactly how many years was Sherlock in active practice?

31. Holmes retired in either late 1903 or early 1904, yet in 1914 he claimed that he was how old?

32. After he gave up his active practice, to where did Holmes retire?

33. Although he himself never married, Holmes once served as best man. Can you name the people whose marriage was made possible because Holmes just happened to be on the scene?

34. What was Holmes given for standing in as a witness, and what did he do with it?

35. Over which section of the paper might we find Holmes poring each morning?

36. Although it does not appear by any means to have been one of his pet phrases, Holmes does during one in-

vestigation exclaim, "Elementary!" What case prompted that now-famous remark?

37. Speaking to Watson, Holmes once stated that he had never felt any emotion "akin to love." Nevertheless, the fact remains that in one of his disguises Holmes became engaged. Can you name the lady who might have become Mrs. Sherlock Holmes?

38. Only one case brought Holmes to the United States. Which one?

39. Who made the wax dummy of Holmes which Count Sylvius nearly destroyed, believing it to be the Master himself?

40. Apparently unconcerned with fashion, Holmes often wore dressing gowns. What are the three colors of Holmes's gowns, and which one did he appear to favor?

41. In his long and illustrious career Holmes handled a great many cases. Within a hundred, how many cases did he claim to have undertaken in "The Final Problem"?

42. Besides his aid to the British government and the Queen, we are told that the Master was of service to at least three other reigning houses in Europe. Which ones were they?

# Answers

1. Montague Street (1)

2. Singlestick, boxing and fencing (3—1 each)

3. Victor Trevor (2)

4. The "old and oily" black clay pipe appears to have been his favorite. (2)

5. Shag (1)

6. The long cherry-wood pipe (3)

7. In the toe of a Persian slipper (1)

8. In the coal scuttle (1)

The Very Worst Tenant—Answers

9.  He claimed to be six feet tall, though Watson said that he was slightly over six feet. (2)

10. Gray (1)

11. "The *Gloria Scott*" (1)

12. A Stradivarius (1)

13. Holmes purchased his violin from a "Jew broker in the Tottenham Court Road for 55 shillings." (2—1 each)

14. Vernet (3)

15. Mycroft (1)

16. The world's first and only *consulting* detective (2)

17. A loaded hunting crop (2)

18. General Gordon and Henry Ward Beecher (2—1 each)

19  Cocaine (1)

20. V.R., for *Victoria Regina* (1)

21. Five (2)

22. "Transfixed by a jack-knife in the very centre of his wooden mantlepiece" (1)

# The Very Worst Tenant—Answers

23. Holmes wrote up "The Adventure of the Blanched Soldier" and "The Adventure of the Lion's Mane." (4—2 each)

24. Captain Basil, Escott the plumber and Altamont (3—1 each)

25. Holmes once stated, "I have been beaten three times by men and once by a woman." (2)

26. The only titles we can be definite about are "The Book of Life," "Upon the Distinction Between the Various Ashes of Tobaccos" and *Practical Handbook of Bee Culture with Some Observations Upon the Segregation of the Queen.* (6—2 each)

27. The only time Holmes's swearing was recorded verbatim was when he exclaimed, "Old woman be damned"; that remark was made in *A Study in Scarlet.* (10—5 each)

28. Twice (2)

29. Wiggins (2)

30. Twenty-three years (2)

31. Sixty (2)

9

The Very Worst Tenant—Answers

32. Sussex Downs (2)

33. Irene Adler and Godfrey Norton (2)

34. Holmes was given a sovereign by Adler, which he meant to wear on his watch chain. (2—1 each)

35. The "Agony" column (1)

36. "The Crooked Man" (5)

37. Agatha, housemaid of Charles Augustus Milverton (5)

38. "His Last Bow" (1)

39. Tavernier, the French modeler, made the statue which Count Sylvius almost coshed. (2)

40. Holmes's gowns were blue, purple and mouse-colored; he was inclined to favor the latter. (4—1 each)

41. One thousand (1)

42. Holmes was of service to the King of Bohemia, the reigning family of Holland, and the King of Scandanavia. (6—2 each)

# Chapter 2
# Good Old Watson

1.    We all know that Dr. Watson's first name is John. What is his middle initial?

2.    Although not as athletic as Holmes, Watson played at least one sport. In which sport did Watson participate?

3.    If you remembered the answer to the last question, you should have no trouble recalling Watson's "old school number." What was it?

4.    From which university did Watson receive his M.D.?

5.    At which hospital did Watson serve as house surgeon?

6.   Where did Watson do his army training prior to his being sent overseas?

7.   Can you name, in order, the two regiments with which Watson served?

8.   Watson was wounded while abroad. In what battle did the eminent physician sustain his injury?

9.   What type of bullet wounded Watson?

10.  Exactly where was the good doctor wounded?

11.  Name the orderly who saved Dr. Watson's life during that infamous exchange.

12.  While serving overseas, he also contracted a disease. What disease befell Watson and caused him to be returned to England?

13.  In what year did the now-famous first meeting between Holmes and his biographer take place?

14.  To whom are we indebted for arranging that most fortuitous introduction?

15.  Following the perfunctory, "How are you?", what were the first words that Sherlock Holmes spoke to Watson?

16.     What kind of animal did Watson claim to have when he first met with his future roommate?

17.     For how many years was Watson "allowed to cooperate with Holmes and keep records of his doings"?

18.     Watson appears to have had practices in three different locations which we can pinpoint. What are they?

19.     From whom did Watson purchase his first practice?

20.     Of the sixty recorded Holmes cases, how many are related by Dr. Watson in the first person?

21.     As tribute to the physician's considerable literary abilities, Holmes often compared Watson to what other literary lion?

22.     Like Holmes, Watson enjoyed a good pipe. To what two types of tobacco was Watson partial?

23.     Speaking of smoking, name Watson's tobacconist, who upon occasion also had Holmes for a client.

24.     What item did Watson inherit from his brother?

25. Watson claimed to have brought two cases to Sherlock's notice. Which ones were they?

26. In describing himself, Watson stated emphatically, "If I have one quality upon earth, it is _____." What was it?

27. On one occasion Watson was shot in the thigh by a murderous blackguard. What case occasioned this misfortune, and who wounded Watson?

28. What case necessitated the good doctor taking a trip to Lausanne as Holmes's agent?

29. On another occasion Watson, acting as Holmes's agent, assumed an alias. Under what *nom de guerre* did Watson operate in "The Illustrious Client"?

30. While using his alias, upon what subject did Watson pretend to be an authority?

31. Where does Watson keep his tin dispatch with the records of his cases with Holmes?

32. While Watson's marital affairs appear complex, we can say with absolute certainty that he married this one woman. Who was she?

33.    What case brought Watson and his wife together?

34.    Due to his association with Holmes, Watson was often forced to neglect his practice. Which two doctors covered for Watson when he was away with Sherlock on a case?

35.    To whom did Watson sell one of his practices?

36.    A rather sociable individual, Watson attended school with a boy who in his later years was to become one of Holmes's clients. What was the boy's name, and which case did he bring to the Master's attention?

37.    In "The Stock-broker's Clerk" Holmes and Watson both used assumed names. Holmes was Mr. Harris; what alias did Watson use?

38.    How many reports did Watson send Holmes while the good doctor was working on *The Hound of the Baskervilles* case?

39.    Although we do not know his name, we are in possession of the first initial of Watson's father. What was it?

40. Watson was partial to what particular piece of music which Holmes would play for him on the violin?

41. Holmes regarded Watson as a dependable individual, and the good doctor appears to have been unusually stolid—with only one noteworthy lapse. Can you recall the case that caused Watson to faint "for the first and last time" in his life?

42. Aside from Holmes, Watson had few friends. Still, he played billiards with one of his companions and consulted another, who worked as a sublibrarian, in connection with a case. Can you remember their names?

43. Chronologically speaking, the last recorded conversation between the great sleuth and his biographer takes place in "His Last Bow." If you recalled Sherlock's first words to Watson, you ought to be able to recall the last words of Watson to Holmes. What were they?

# Answers

1.      H. (1)

2.      Watson played rugby for the Blackheath Football Club. (1)

3.      31 (3)

4.      The University of London (2)

5.      At St. Bartholomew's Hospital (2)

6.      Netley (2)

7.      Watson served first with the Fifth Northumberland Fusiliers and he was later assigned to the Berkshires. (4—2 each)

## Good Old Watson—Answers

8. Watson was wounded in the Battle of Maiwand. (1)

9. A Jezail bullet (1)

10. Here we have a bit of a mystery. In *A Study in Scarlet,* Watson claims to have been wounded in the shoulder. However, in *The Sign of Four*, he states that he was wounded in the leg. (4—2 each)

11. Murray (3)

12. Watson contracted enteric fever, more commonly known as typhoid fever. (2)

13. 1881 (1)

14. Young Stamford (1)

15. Holmes uttered the now-famous line, "You have been in Afghanistan, I perceive." (3)

16. Watson told Holmes that he had a bull pup, but since no mention is ever made of the animal again, it has been conjectured that Watson was speaking metaphorically; saying that he kept a bull pup may have been Watson's way of telling Holmes that the good doctor possessed a quick temper. (3)

17. Seventeen (3)

18

18. Paddington, Kensington and Queen Anne Street (3—1 each)

19. Dr. Farquhar (2)

20. Fifty-six (4)

21. James Boswell, the biographer of Dr. Samuel Johnson (1)

22. In his "bachelor days" and in his later years, Watson smoked an Arcardia mixture; in between, he appears to have favored Ship's. (2—1 each)

23. Bradley (2)

24. A "50-guinea" watch (2)

25. Watson claims to have introduced only "two problems": "that of Mr. Hatherley's thumb [which we know as "The Adventure of the Engineer's Thumb"] and that of Colonel Warburton's madness." (2—1 each)

26. Common sense (2)

27. Watson was shot by James Winter, alias "Killer" Evans alias Moorecroft alias John Garrideb, during "The Adventure of the Three Garridebs" (2—1 each)

# Good Old Watson—Answers

28. "The Disappearance of Lady Frances Carfax" (2)

29. Dr. Hill Barton (5)

30. Chinese pottery (2)

31. In the vaults of Cox and Company at Charing Cross (2)

32. Mary Morstan (1)

33. *The Sign of Four* (1)

34. Anstruther and Jackson (4—2 each)

35. Watson sold his Kensington practice to a Dr. Verner, who apparently purchased it with money provided by his distant cousin . . . Sherlock Holmes. (3)

36. Percy "Tadpole" Phelps brought "The Naval Treaty" to the attention of Holmes. (2—1 each)

37. Watson was Mr. Price. (5)

38. Two (1)

39. It was Watson's own middle initial: H. (2)

40. Mendelssohn's *Lieder* (5)

20

41. Watson fainted during "The Adventure of the Empty House" when he learned that his best friend was somehow still alive. (2)

42. Watson played billiards with Thurston prior to the commencement of "The Dancing Men," and he consulted Lomax in connection with "The Adventure of the Illustrious Client." (2—1 each)

43. Watson's last recorded words to Holmes are "I think not, Holmes. It is very warm!" (2)

# Chapter 3
# He Is the Napoleon of Crime

1.   What was the evil Professor Moriarty's first name?

2.   Though long Holmes's antagonist, the Professor only appears as a character in a single canonical work. Which one?

3.   Despite the fact that we do not know a great deal about Moriarty's family, we do have some facts at our disposal. For example, we know the name of one of his two brothers. What is that name?

4.   While we do not know the name of the Professor's other brother, we are told that he worked in the west of England. What was his occupation?

5.    Like Holmes, Moriarty was an author. Can you remember the names of the two works that the Professor penned?

6.    Prior to embarking upon his life of crime, Moriarty held a chair at a small university in England. What was his annual salary?

7.    After things became a bit too hot at the university, Moriarty "resigned." What profession did he adopt as a cover for his illegal activities?

8.    We know that Moriarty visited Holmes once at Baker Street. How many times did the Master visit the home of his archenemy?

9.    Holmes once managed to subvert one of Moriarty's agents, who would sometimes warn Holmes of crimes about to be committed. What name did this agent use in dealing with Holmes?

10.    This agent once sent the Master a cipher warning him about a man in danger. Unfortunately, he was unable to send Holmes the key to the cipher. In a brilliant demonstration of deductive reasoning, Holmes still managed to locate the necessary volume. What was the book's title?

11.    In the cipher sent by Moriarty's agent, only two words were used. Can you remember them?

12.   Acting on Holmes's suggestion, Scotland Yard took an interest in the Professor. What inspector visited the Professor?

13.   When the man from the Yard paid Moriarty a visit, they discussed neither crime nor Holmes. What, in fact, did these two potential adversaries discuss so amiably?

14.   Moriarty had a painting by what artist adorning the wall of his study?

15.   To what other legendary English criminal did Holmes compare the nefarious Professor Moriarty?

16.   How many bank accounts does Holmes tell us the Professor kept—at least minimally?

17.   Just as we have come to associate the phrase "Elementary, my dear Watson" with Holmes, so too did the archvillain have a favorite expression. What was it?

18.   When Holmes and Watson sought refuge on the continent, Holmes began the trip incognito. What disguise did the Master assume to escape the evil Professor and his henchmen?

19.   At what historic city did Holmes and Watson leave their train in what proved to be

a vain attempt to elude the pursuing Professor?

20. What is the name of the village which Holmes and Watson reached on May 3, 1891, in their flight from Moriarty?

21. What was the name of the hotel in which they stayed that night and to which Watson was subsequently decoyed by the Professor?

22. Who was the proprietor of this fine hostelry?

23. On May 4, a fateful date for both the Master and Moriarty, Holmes and Watson set out for what village?

24. Enroute to that village, they made a side trip to the place where Holmes and Moriarty had their final confrontation. Where did that momentous meeting occur?

25. How did Moriarty's hidden associate try to kill Holmes after he witnessed Holmes vanquish the "Napoleon of crime"?

26. When Watson returned to the place where he had left Holmes, what two items —excluding Holmes's letter—did he find?

27.   In his "final" letter, Holmes wrote Watson that he had left papers for someone in pigeonhole M in a blue envelope inscribed "Moriarty." Whom were the papers for?

28.   Since Moriarty never engaged in any criminal activities himself, he assembled a top-flight organization. Who was the Professor's first lieutenant and chief of staff?

29.   What amount was that individual paid by the Professor as an annual salary?

30.   What was that person's favorite weapon?

31.   Who constructed that weapon at the order of Professor Moriarty and from what physical disability did that individual suffer?

32.   What is the period of time when Holmes was in hiding from the remainder of Moriarty's gang commonly called, and approximately how many years did that period last?

33.   During that period of time, what name did Holmes use to travel?

34.   Who was Holmes's only confidante during his extended absence from Baker Street?

35. When he returned to London, Holmes, disguised as an old bibliophile, literally bumped into Watson. Can you recall the names of any of the books that he was carrying because of his disguise?

36. Who made the wax bust of Holmes which Moriarty's aide tried to dispatch with his devilish weapon?

37. Can you name at least one other person —two are mentioned by name—who was murdered by Moriarty's first lieutenant?

38. Like his evil superior, Moriarty's chief underling was also an author. Can you name the two books he wrote?

39. What self-defense technique did Holmes employ when he finally overcame Moriarty?

40. What was the actual name of the house which gave the title to "The Adventure of the Empty House"?

41. What case prompted Holmes to remark, "I can tell a Moriarty when I see one"?

42. What term did Holmes use in referring to Moriarty's captured chief of staff? Hint: Holmes called him an old _____.

# Answers

1. James (1)

2. "The Final Problem" (1)

3. Colonel James Moriarty—the fact that both the Professor and his brother share a common first name has prompted some to suggest that James Moriarty was a compound surname. (1)

4. Moriarty's other brother worked as a station master. (2)

5. Moriarty wrote "A Treatise Upon the Binomial Theorem" and *The Dynamics of an Asteroid*. (4—2 each for exact titles)

6.      Seven hundred pounds (4)

7.      Moriarty became an army coach. (2)

8.      Prior to the visit at Baker Street, Holmes had never met Moriarty. However, he admitted to being in the Professor's rooms on three separate occasions—twice legally and once illegally. (2)

9.      Fred Porlock (3)

10.     *Whitaker's Almanac* (5)

11.     *Birlstone* was mentioned twice, and *Douglas* was used once. (2—1 each)

12.     Inspector MacDonald (2)

13.     They discussed eclipses. (3)

14.     Jean Baptiste Greuze (3)

15.     Jonathan Wild (5)

16.     Six (3)

17.     "Dear me, Mr. Holmes! Dear me!" (2)

18.     Holmes began the trip disguised as an Italian priest. (1)

19.     Canterbury (2)

# He Is the Napoleon of Crime—Answers

20.     Meiringen (1)

21.     They stayed at the Englischer Hof. (1)

22.     Peter Steiler the elder (2)

23.     Rosenlaui (2)

24.     Reichenbach Falls (1)

25.     Moriarty's associate, perched high up the Falls, tried to drop rocks on Holmes and thus cause him as well to fall into the abyss. (2)

26.     Watson found Holmes's alpenstock and silver cigarette case. (2—1 each)

27.     Inspector Patterson (3)

28.     Colonel Sebastian Moran (1)

29.     Moran was paid six thousand pounds annually. (3)

30.     Moran preferred an air-gun. (1)

31.     Von Herder, the German mechanic, was blind. (4—2 each)

32.     "The Great Hiatus" lasted nearly three years—from May 1891 until April 1894. (2—1 each)

33. "You may have heard of the remarkable explorations of a Norwegian named Sigerson." (2)

34. His brother Mycroft (1)

35. *The Origin of Tree Worship, British Birds, Catullus* and *The Holy War* (4—1 each)

36. Monsieur Oscar Meunier of Grenoble made the bust which Moran shot. (3)

37. Hon. Ronald Adair and Mrs. Stewart of Laudor, in 1887 (2—give yourself 2 bonus points if you named both)

38. Moran authored *Heavy Game of the Himalayas* (1881) and *Three Months in the Jungle* (1884) (6—3 each)

39. *Baritsu* (2)

40. Camden House (2)

41. The case was *The Valley of Fear,* but the remark was occasioned when Holmes learned that John Douglas had been lost overboard in a gale near St. Helena. (2)

42. Holmes called Moran an old *shikari,* a Hindu word meaning "hunter." (3)

# Chapter 4
# The Game Is Afoot

1.  Watson once wrote, "To Sherlock Holmes she is always *the* woman." About whom was he speaking?

2.  What invention was outlined in the Bruce-Partington plans?

3.  What was written in blood on the wall in *A Study in Scarlet*?

4.  Whose house did Holmes enter in the guise of a Nonconformist clergyman?

5.  Which case came to an unlikely conclusion when Holmes put a "large bath sponge" to its proper use?

6.  Whose hat, which accidentally fell into Holmes's hands, proved an invaluable clue in locating and recovering the Countess of Morcar's missing gem?

7.  What specific action was Violet Hunter required to take if she wished to obtain an extremely lucrative position as a governess?

8.  In "The Yellow Face" Holmes remarked, "There's blackmail in it, or I'm much mistaken." As we know, this was one of the few times that the Master was "much mistaken." What word did Sherlock instruct Watson to whisper to him if he ever began getting "a little overconfident" in his powers?

9.  In which case did the height of an elm tree figure prominently in the Master's calculations?

10. What "clue" did Jonas Oldacre leave as evidence of his death which had just the opposite effect, firmly convincing Holmes that the man was still alive and in hiding?

11. In which case did Holmes encounter special horseshoes designed to make horses' hoofprints look like the hoofprints of cows?

12. What make of pencil figured to a degree in aiding Holmes in "The Adventure of the Three Students"?

13. Who died uttering the words, "The professor—it was she"?

14. Bell pulls provided Holmes with important clues in two cases. In one case the bell pull was a dummy; in the other the rope had been "ripped" down, but no one had heard the bell sound. Which cases depended upon Holmes's correctly sounding out the meaning of these two clues?

15. Although nothing could be more incongruous than voodoo and Victorian England, the fact remains that Holmes handled a case in which there were hints of voodooism. Which case was it?

16. Who made the brand of cigarettes of which Holmes smoked so many and whose ashes enabled him to determine that someone was hiding in Professor Coram's room?

17. Prior to checking out the clue provided by the cigarette ashes, Holmes had pretty much ascertained that his hypothesis was correct. What action of the Professor's had aroused Holmes's suspicions and pointed him in the right direction?

18. What did Holmes discover in the garden outside Mortimer Tregennis's window that put him on the track of the man who had caused Mortimer's death?

19. What was the combination to the safe in Von Bork's library which Holmes was able to elicit from the master spy?

20. Animals figure prominently in a number of Holmes's cases, as we shall see in Chapter 6; however, right now, can you name the two cases in which the sudden lameness of apparently healthy animals pointed the Master in the direction of the solution?

21. In which case did the fictitious Dr. Lysander Starr help Holmes to trap a villain?

22. What color was the first boot of Sir Henry Baskerville's to disappear?

23. In which of Holmes's many cases did a sleeping watchdog furnish an invaluable clue as to the identity of the felon?

24. Holmes was able to find out the truth about Jack Stapleton because the criminal slipped. What vital piece of background information did Stapleton reveal about himself to Watson which Holmes, in turn, capitalized upon?

25. In *The Valley of Fear,* what item—conspicuously absent from the scene of the crime—provided Holmes with a healthy clue to the correct solution?

26. In which of his cases did Sherlock discern a clue by noting the presence of beeswax in only a single wineglass?

27. Which of Holmes's adventures—many of which involved events best described as *outre*—brought him into contact with a pair of freshly severed human ears?

28. What was the name of the firm that recommended Mr. Robert Ferguson to Holmes and thus was responsible—at least indirectly—for the Master's meeting with "The Sussex Vampire"?

29. Where had Irene Adler hidden the photograph that she was holding against the King of Bohemia?

30. What unusual weapon was found in John Straker's hand and so helped Holmes to learn what had actually happened to Silver Blaze?

31. In dealing with the death of Colonel James Barclay, Holmes told Watson, "That one word should have told me the whole story had I been the ideal reasoner

which you are so fond of depicting." What was the word whose significance escaped the Master?

32. What two items did Jonathan Small's companion leave at Bartholomew Sholto's residence?

33. In which case were "an odd volume of Pope's *Homer*, two plated candlesticks, an ivory letter weight, a small oak barometer, and a ball of twine" stolen? Holmes immediately recognized the theft for what it was: a blind.

34. In connection with which case did Holmes almost fail to appreciate the significance of a remark about a coffin "being out of the ordinary"?

35. Occasionally Holmes slipped up; after all, he was only human. Which two cases might be considered absolute failures from Sherlock's point of view?

36. Only two of Holmes's clients were murdered after they came to him for help. Who were they?

# Answers

1.     Irene Adler (1)

2.     A submarine (1)

3.     *RACHE*, a red herring if ever there was one (1)

4.     Irene Adler's (2)

5.     "The Man with the Twisted Lip" (1)

6.     Henry Baker's (2)

7.     Violet Hunter was asked to cut her long chestnut hair. (2)

8.     Watson was to whisper "Norbury"; this was where Mr. Grant Munro lived. (5)

9. "The Musgrave Ritual" (3)

10. Oldacre left a thumbprint near his hatrack, which had not been there when Holmes inspected the premises the prior day. (3)

11. "The Adventure of the Priory School" (3)

12. A pencil made by Johann Faber. (4)

13. Willoughby Smith (2)

14. "The Adventure of the Speckled Band" and "The Adventure of the Abbey Grange" (4—2 each)

15. "The Adventure of Wisteria Lodge" (2)

16. Ionides of Alexandria (5)

17. Holmes learned that Professor Coram, a bedridden man, was eating more than he usually did. (3)

18. Red gravel (3)

19. August 1914 (3)

20. In "Silver Blaze" Holmes discovered the lamed sheep on which Straker had been practicing, and in "The Sussex Vampire" the Master deduced that the culprit had been testing the poison on the family dog. (4—2 each)

The Game Is Afoot—Answers

21. "The Adventure of the Three Garridebs" (2)

22. Brown or tan—since it is referred to as both, either is acceptable. (1)

23. "Silver Blaze" (2)

24. Stapleton told Watson that he, Stapleton, had been a schoolmaster. (5)

25. A dumbbell (2)

26. "The Adventure of the Abbey Grange" (2)

27. "The Adventure of the Cardboard Box" (2)

28. Morrison, Morrison, and Dodd (5)

29. The photograph was concealed in a recess behind a sliding panel just above the right bell pull. (5—only if your description was exact)

30. A cataract knife (2)

31. The key word was *David*. (5)

32. A stone "instrument" was left in Sholto's study, and Holmes found a pouch containing thorns on the roof. (2—1 each)

## The Game Is Afoot—Answers

33. "The Reigate Squires" (2)

34. "The Disappearance of Lady Frances Carfax" (3)

35. "A Scandal in Bohemia" and "The Yellow Face" would have to be listed among the Master's disappointing showings. (2—1 each)

36. John Openshaw and Hilton Cubitt (4—2 each)

# Chapter 5
# A Colorful Career

1. Exactly how many cases in the canon contain a specific color in their titles?

2. What was the first Sherlock Holmes novel?

3. Watson once discovered Holmes posing as an old opium addict. What was the name of the opium den where this chance meeting occurred?

4. In which Holmes story did the notorious Ku Klux Klan figure prominently?

5. What precious gem did the Countess of Morcar possess?

6.  As you know, houses in England are quite often given names. What was the colorful appellation assigned to Jephro Rucastle's estate?

7.  Who won the Wessex Cup in 1890, an outcome influenced in no little part by the work of Holmes?

8.  Holmes, as we are told, often used disguises. What alias did the Master use while working on the case of "Black Peter"?

9.  What color was the famed "pearl of the Borgias," which the Master was instrumental in recovering?

10. By what colorful nickname was J. Neil Gibson more commonly known?

11. Who was in love with Lady Frances Carfax and in part responsible for solving the case of her disappearance?

12. From what deadly organization with a colorful epithet were Gennaro and Emilia Lucca fleeing?

13. One of Holmes's greatest errors involved the work he did for Mr. Grant Munro. Which case did Munro bring to the Master's attention?

14. What was the "colorful" name of the local officer at Birlstone in *The Valley of Fear*?

15. What type of detective was Birdy Edwards, a.k.a. John Douglas?

16. What was Willoughby Smith clutching in his right hand when his body was discovered?

17. Who was known in his youth as Black Jack of Ballarat?

18. In "The Dying Detective" Holmes received a small ivory box. What color was it?

19. Whom did Holmes have in mind when he referred to the "king of the blackmailers"?

20. By what popular name was *The Sporting Times* more commonly called?

21. From what disease did Roger Baskerville die?

22. One of the adventures mentioned by Watson but never related involved Holmes's handling of a case concerned with a leech. What color was the repugnant worm?

23. What colorful term might be used to describe Godfrey Staunton, Harold Stackhurst and young Gilchrist?

24. What was the distinctive hair tint shared by the Misses Hunter and Rucastle? Be as exact as possible.

25. What colorful clue, first observed by Hall Pycroft, led Holmes to suspect that Arthur and Harry Pinner were actually the same man?

26. At what colorful inn did Holmes and Watson stay while they were investigating the mystery of Shoscombe Old Place?

27. What was "Black Gorgiano's" first name?

28. Violet Hunter was asked by Jephro Rucastle to wear a blue dress. Specifically, what shade of blue was the gown which Miss Hunter was asked to don?

29. What were the colors of King's Pyland stables?

30. What color(s) was the safe in Charles Augustus Milverton's room which Holmes attempted to burgle?

31. What were the colors of San Pedro?

32. Who owned the fifth bust of the Little Corporal which Beppo stole and which Holmes caught him destroying? Give the first and last names.

33. What color was the lead pencil which provided Holmes with a clue in "The Three Students"?

34. Where did Holmes and Watson dine while they were searching for the Bruce-Partington plans?

35. What color was the specimen of Chinese pottery Holmes gave Watson to use in "The Illustrious Client"? Be exact.

36. What color was the bottle of prussic acid which Eugenia Ronder sent Holmes?

37. What is the only case in the canon which actually contains the word *colour* in its title?

38. What shade of paint did Josiah Amberley use on the interior of his home in a vain effort to conceal the odor of gas?

39. What inn did Holmes suggest Watson ought to have visited in an effort to obtain information about the aforementioned Mr. Amberley?

40. What color was the cover of Baron Gruner's book of women, a volume which Holmes tried to seize without the Baron's permission?

41.   What color was Toby the hound, used by Holmes in *The Sign of Four*?

42.   Who was the indigo planter who hired Jonathan Small after Small had lost his leg?

43.   During *The Hound of the Baskervilles* Watson saw an unknown man—later discovered to be the Master—on the summit of what tinted tor?

44.   Specifically, what color was the "hound of hell" devised by Stapleton? You get full credit only if you can provide the adjective that goes with the color.

45.   What type of perfume did Beryl Stapleton favor which Holmes detected on the note that she had sent to Sir Henry Baskerville?

46.   What colorful nickname was sometimes applied to John McGinty?

47.   Name Holmes's client who was being blackmailed by Charles Augustus Milverton.

# Answers

1. Ten, if you consider copper a color, which we do (5)

2. *A Study in Scarlet* (1)

3. The Bar of Gold (2)

4. "The Five Orange Pips" (1)

5. The Blue Carbuncle (1)

6. Rucastle owned The Copper Beeches. (2)

7. Silver Blaze (1)

8. Holmes masqueraded as Captain Basil. (2)

# A Colorful Career—Answers

9.      Black (1)

10.     J. Neil Gibson, the "Gold King," was "the greatest gold-mining magnate in the world." (1)

11.     The Hon. Philip Green (2)

12.     The Red Circle was the group that terrorized the Luccas. (1)

13.     "The Yellow Face" (1)

14.     The local officer at Birlstone was named White Mason. (3)

15.     Edwards was a *Pink*erton. (Sorry about that!) (1)

16.     Smith was found grasping a golden pince-nez—hence the title. (1)

17.     John Turner (2)

18.     Actually it was two colors: black and white. (2)

19.     Charles Augustus Milverton (2)

20.     That particular publication was affectionately known as the "Pink 'Un." (3)

21.     Yellow fever (1)

50

# A Colorful Career—Answers

22.    It was a red leech. (3)

23.    They were all Blues, meaning that they were varsity athletes at either Oxford or Cambridge. (2)

24.    Their hair was a distinctive shade of chestnut brown. (2—if you merely said brown, give yourself 1 and see Chapter 4, question 8)

25.    A "badly stuffed gold tooth" (3)

26.    They stayed at The Green Dragon. (3)

27.    Giuseppe (2)

28.    "Electric blue" was the term used to describe the dress. (2)

29.    Black and red (4)

30.    Green and gold (2)

31.    Green and white (2)

32.    Mr. Josiah Brown (5)

33.    Blue (2)

34.    *Gold*ini's Restaurant (4—at this point, you should have expected that!)

35.    It was a deep blue. (1)

# A Colorful Career—Answers

36. Blue (1)

37. "The Adventure of the Retired *Colour-man*" (1)

38. Green (2)

39. The Blue Anchor (5)

40. The book was brown leather with the Baron's coat of arms in gold on the cover. (2)

41. Toby was brown and white. (2)

42. Abel White (2)

43. Black Tor (1)

44. The hound was described as being coal black. (3)

45. White Jessamine (5)

46. "Black Jack" (1)

47. Lady Eva *Black*well (2)

# Chapter 6
# Silver Blaze *et al.*

1.  Which did Holmes tell Watson was "the deadliest snake in India"?

2.  What type of animal swallowed the Countess of Morcar's precious stone?

3.  Holmes once solved a case involving an *ichneumon*. As what is an *ichneumon* more commonly known, and what was this one's name?

4.  Dr. Grimesby Roylott allowed two animals to roam freely over the grounds of his estate. What were they?

5.  What was the villainous Don Murillo's bestial epithet?

6.    Who sired Silver Blaze?

7.    What type of animal was responsible for mutilating Eugenia Ronder's face and what was the beast's name?

8.    Jephro Rucastle and Robert Ferguson owned different dogs with the same name. What common name did their pets share?

9.    In "The Adventure of the Missing Three-Quarter" Holmes called in the pride of the local draghounds. What was the name of that canine sleuth?

10.   What was the name of the inn owned by Reuben Hayes?

11.   Can you recall the name of the horse that won the Derby in 1902?

12.   What was the last name of the ferocious Kitty, who threw vitriol in Baron Gruner's face?

13.   In "The Adventure of the Creeping Man," what type of dog did Professor Presbury own, and what was its name?

14.   *Cynea capillata* is more commonly known as what?

15.   What was John Douglas's real name?

16.     According to the legend which Dr. Mortimer related to Holmes and Watson, who was the first victim of "the hound of the Baskervilles"?

17.     The hound used by Stapleton to resurrect the legend was a mixed breed. What breeds were mixed?

18.     Who owns the only Airedale terrier mentioned in the entire canon?

19.     Stapleton tried to convince Watson the noises they heard on the Grimpen Mire were the calls of a bird. What type of bird did he blame for the sounds?

20.     What was the name of the hotel in Winchester where Holmes met with Miss Hunter during "The Copper Beeches"?

21.     What animals' heads appeared on the Baskervilles' coat of arms?

22.     Were you paying attention? One of the books Holmes carried in his disguise as an old bibliophile had a bestial title. What was it?

23.     In "His Last Bow" Holmes told Watson that as Altamont, he had joined an Irish secret society in what city?

24.     Enoch Drebber wore a gold pin in the shape of what animal?

25.     In addition to the *ichneumon*, what pet did Henry Woods own?

26.     What "trained" animal goes with the untold tale of the "politician and the lighthouse"?

27.     Another untold tale concerns itself with a "giant" rat from a foreign country. Where did this overgrown rodent hail from?

28.     For what special breed of dog was Lady Beatrice Falder renowned?

29.     Speaking of dogs, what type of canine did Mrs. Hudson, Holmes's landlady, own?

30.     Name the horse scratched from the Wessex Cup.

31.     What was the name of the horse who finished second to Silver Blaze in the Wessex Cup?

32.     In addition to the answer to the above question, Silver Blaze ran against four other horses. How many can you name?

33.     What was the heraldic sign of the Capus family of Birlstone?

34.     What was the name of the mine managed by Josiah H. Dunn in *The Valley of Fear*?

35.     Where was Teddy Baldwin staying prior to his attempt on the life of John Douglas?

36.     Irene Adler lived in Briony Lodge in St. John's Wood. On what street did Holmes find her house?

37.     What type of dog, owned by Victor Trevor, bit Holmes while he was in college?

38.     Speaking of birds, can you name the villain, brought to justice by Holmes, who once loosed a cat in an aviary?

39.     What inn was closest to the Priory School?

40.     Holmes was once asked by Lord Bellinger and the Rt. Hon. Trelawney Hope to recover a certain long, pale-blue envelope which had been sealed with red wax. What animal figure was imprinted in the sealing wax?

41.     Where did Holmes and Watson stay while they were working on "The Adventure of Wisteria Lodge"?

42.     What was the unflattering name of Shinwell Johnson, the reformed criminal who sometimes aided Holmes?

43.    In which case did Holmes put a terrier out of its misery with pills which might later have been used as evidence?

44.    Where did Jefferson Hope have a mule and two horses waiting as he plotted how he and the Ferriers could escape the Avenging Angels?

45.    How did Jonathan Small lose his leg?

46.    Where did Stapleton purchase the dog which he turned into the spectral "hound of the Baskervilles"?

47.    How old was Silver Blaze at the time of his disappearance?

# Answers

1.  The swamp adder earned that distinction in the Master's mind. (1)

2.  A bar-tailed goose (1)

3.  An *ichneumon* is more commonly known as a mongoose, and the one owned by Henry Woods was called Teddy. (4—2 each)

4.  A baboon and a cheetah (2—1 each)

5.  "The Tiger of San Pedro." (1)

6.  Silver Blaze was sired by Isonomy; in some editions this appears as Sonomy. (3)

7.  A lion, "Sahara King," mauled the troubled lady. (2—1 each)

8.  Rucastle's mastiff and Ferguson's spaniel were both named Carlo. (2)

9.  Pompey (2)

10. Reuben Hayes was the proprietor of The Fighting Cock. (2)

11. Shoscombe Prince owns that distinction. (1)

12. The firey female's name was Kitty Winter. (1)

13. Professor Presbury owned a wolfhound named Roy. (4—2 each)

14. Lion's mane (1)

15. Birdy Edwards (1)

16. According to legend, the infamous Hugo Baskerville was responsible for instigating all the trouble. (1)

17. Stapleton's hound was a cross between a bloodhound and a mastiff. (2)

18. Fitzroy McPherson (3)

19. He said the noises were made by the very rare and almost extinct bittern. (3)

20. Holmes met with Miss Hunter at The Black Swan. (2)

21. The Baskerville coat of arms featured boars' heads. (3)

22. *British Birds* was the book's title. (5—if you answered this incorrectly, you violated one of the Master's basic tenets: you saw, but you did not observe)

23. Buffalo, New York (1)

24. A bulldog (3)

25. Woods kept a defanged cobra, which Teddy caught "every night to please the folks in the canteen." (1)

26. A cormorant (2)

27. Holmes was involved in a case that dealt with the giant rat of Sumatra. Watson makes it clear that this is a case for which the world is not yet ready. (2)

28. Lady Beatrice bred the famous Shoscombe spaniels, "the most exclusive breed in England." (1)

29. Mrs. Hudson owned "an ageing terrier." (2)

30. Colonel Ross scratched his horse Bayard. (5)

31. Desborough finished in second place to the favored Silver Blaze. (3)

32. Besides Desborough, Silver Blaze competed against Iris, Pugilist, Rasper and The Negro. (4—1 each)

33. A rampant lion (3—if you merely said a lion, give yourself only 1)

34. Dunn was the manager of Crow Hill. (3)

35. Baldwin was staying at the Eagle Commercial in Tunbridge Wells. (1)

36. Serpentine Avenue (3)

37. Trevor owned a bulldog. (1)

38. Jonas Oldacre (2)

39. The Red Bull (2)

40. "A crouching lion" (1)

41. They stayed at The Bull in Esher in Surrey. (2)

42.    Holmes's assistant had the unflattering nickname "Porky." (1)

43.    *A Study in Scarlet* (1)

44.    "Eagle Canon" (1)

45.    He lost it to a crocodile in the Ganges. (1)

46.    Stapleton bought the hound at Ross and Mangles on Fulham Road. (5)

47.    He was five. (2)

# Chapter 7
# All That Glitters Is Not Gold

1.   Though a rather uncommon stone today, beryls are mentioned in connection with at least three of Holmes's exploits. How many of the exploits can you name?

2.   What was the name of the largest diamond in the Agra Treasure?

3.   Enoch Drebber was found wearing a gold pin in the shape of an animal (see Chapter 6, question 26). What type of stones did the pin have for eyes?

4.   Approximately how many pounds sterling did Thaddeus Sholto claim the Agra Treasure was worth?

5.   What did Holmes receive as a reward for his help in recovering the Bruce-Partington Plans and who presented it to him?

6.   Holmes once refused an emerald snake ring offered him by the King of Bohemia. What did he request in lieu of the ring?

7.   What type of jewel did Mary Morstan receive in the post each year?

8.   Exactly what type of gem was the Mazarin Stone, and who was responsible for its theft?

9.   Which of the Master's cases are named after specific gemstones?

10.   Within one hundred, how many stones did Jonathan Small list by number as being in the Agra Treasure?

11.   What did Small do with the vast majority of the stones?

12.   Holmes once received a remarkable "brilliant ring" from one of Europe's reigning families. Which family gave it to him?

13.   What was the exact number of beryls in the beryl coronet?

14.   How many stones were broken off the coronet in the struggle for its possession?

15. Aside from its size, the Mazarin Stone was unique because of its unusual tint. What color was the Mazarin Stone?

16. Who owned a silver and brilliant pendant that was found pawned "at Bovington's in the Westminster Road"?

17. Okay, gold also glitters, so here are a few questions having to do with that precious substance. What is the only case in the canon that contains the word *gold* in its title?

18. Who presented Holmes with a gold snuff-box in gratitude for Sherlock's fine work on a case?

19. What type of jewel was in the "centre of the lid" of the snuffbox?

20. Which of Holmes's adversaries lived in a house that had been built by a South African gold king?

21. What color is an ordinary carbuncle?

22. What two types of rings did John Douglas place on the fingers of the dead Teddy Baldwin?

23. How much did the legendary Blue Carbuncle weigh, and where was it found?

24. For how much of a loan was the beryl coronet left as security?

25. How much did it cost Sherlock Holmes to buy back the missing beryls from the damaged coronet?

26. Which case brought Holmes into direct contact with the crown that "once encircled the brows of the royal Stuarts"?

27. Who owned the black pearl of the Borgias when it was stolen from his room at the Dacre Hotel?

28. Who was found dead wearing a gold ring with a masonic device?

29. Who was the merchant who brought the great Agra Treasure into the fort and was subsequently stabbed to death?

30. Name the jeweler who was going to smuggle the Mazarin Stone out of England.

31. Where did Godfrey Norton stop—presumably to buy a ring for his wedding to Irene Adler—just before he proceeded to the church?

32. What was the approximate value of the Mazarin Stone, according to Dr. Watson?

# Answers

1. "A Scandal in Bohemia," *The Sign of Four* and "The Adventure of the Beryl Coronet." There was also a Beryl in *The Hound of the Baskervilles;* however, she was something less than a jewel. (3—1 each)

2. The Great Mogul (5)

3. Rubies (2)

4. Thaddeus stated that his brother had estimated "the value of the jewels at not less than half a million sterling." (3)

5. Holmes received an emerald tie pin, and although Holmes does not give her name, Watson informs us that the detective had

spent the day at Windsor, from whence he returned with the pin. It seems safe and logical to assume that the "certain gracious lady" alluded to by Holmes was no less than Queen Victoria herself. (4—2 each)

6. A photograph of Irene Adler in evening dress (2)

7. A pearl (1)

8. The Mazarin Stone was stolen by Count Negretto Sylvius. (4—2 each)

9. "The Adventure of the Blue Carbuncle" and "The Adventure of the Mazarin Stone" (2—1 each)

10. There were 721 stones by count and "approximately 300 pearls," making for an approximate count of 1021. (5—if you got the exact number, award yourself a bonus 10 and share a nip with Athelney Jones)

11. Small threw the gems in the Thames as he fled from Holmes. (2)

12. Holmes received the ring from the reigning family of Holland. (3)

13. Thirty-nine (2)

14. Three (2)

# All That Glitters Is Not Gold—Answers

15. It was tinted yellow. (1)

16. Lady Frances Carfax (1)

17. "The Adventure of the Golden Pince-Nez" (1)

18. The King of Bohemia (2)

19. A great amethyst (2)

20. Baron Adelbert Gruner (3)

21. Deep red with a mixture of scarlet (2)

22. A nugget ring and a snake ring (2—1 each)

23. Weighing forty grams, the gem had been found in the Amoy River in southern China. (10—5 each)

24. 50,000 pounds (3)

25. 3,000 pounds (3)

26. "The Musgrave Ritual" (2)

27. The Prince of Colonna (5)

28. Enoch Drebber (2)

29. Achmet (3)

# All That Glitters Is Not Gold—Answers

30.  Van Sedder (3)

31.  Gross and Hankey's (5)

32.  100,000 pounds (10)

# Chapter 8
# The Yard

1.  Here's a real toughie. As you know, Scotland Yard inspectors figure in a number of Holmes's cases. Within three, how many different Scotland Yard inspectors are mentioned by name throughout the canon?

2.  Although the Master worked with a great many Scotland Yard officials, only two of them shared a common last name. What was the surname shared by those Yarders?

3.  Who was the Scotland Yard inspector with whom Sherlock most frequently worked?

4.  On how many cases did they collaborate?

5.     Competition among the Yarders was fierce. Who was the previous inspector's rival?

6.     On how many cases did Holmes work with this man?

7.     Holmes and the previous two inspectors worked together on only a single case. What adventure forced the Master to join forces "with the best of a bad lot"?

8.     Although dominated by men, the Yard apparently had its share of women on staff. Unfortunately, only one tale mentions an unnamed policewoman on the job. In which tale does this distaff detective appear?

9.     We do not know the "tenacious" Inspector Lestrade's first name, yet we do know his first initial. What is it?

10.    For approximately how many years did Lestrade—with Holmes's help—protect the citizens of London from all types of ne'er-do-wells? In other words, how long was he on the force (within three years)?

11.    To which police station did Holmes and Watson travel to inspect the saucy-tongued mendicant Hugh Boone?

12. What member of Scotland Yard once referred to Sherlock Holmes as "Mr. Theorist"?

13. Scotland Yard is divided up into detectives and constables. What was the name of the constable who blew the whistle—literally —on *A Study in Scarlet*?

14. What was the name of the officer on duty at the home of Eduardo Lucas who was outwitted by Lady Hilda Trelawney Hope?

15. Though Holmes often worked with the Scotland Yarders, he did not hold a very high opinion of their abilities as detectives. Which villain disparagingly referred to the Master as a "Scotland Yard jack-in-office"—a remark to which Holmes appears to have taken some exception?

16. Holmes aided many C.I.D. men, but there was one young investigator in whose career the Master evidenced a special interest. Who was this fortunate individual?

17. Which case did this aspiring inspector describe as his "first big chance"?

18. Can you remember the case which this same detective recommended to the attention of Holmes, but in which he took no active part himself?

19. While we do not know Inspector Lestrade's Christian name, we do know Inspector Gregson's. What was his first name?

20. Can you remember the two divisions of Scotland Yard that were singled out by their letters in the canon?

21. Besides Bow Street, name the two police stations mentioned by name in the canon.

22. Name the item from a case on which Holmes worked that you might see on a visit to the Scotland Yard Museum.

23. Oddly enough, in one case Lestrade was "retained" by a client; however, he, "being rather puzzled . . . referred the case to" Holmes. Which case is it that has some experts believing that Lestrade went into private practice for a time?

24. Stanley Hopkins consulted Holmes with regard to three separate murder cases. Can you name the victims whose deaths so bewildered the C.I.D. man?

25. Inspector Bradstreet worked on only three cases with Holmes. How many of them can you remember? Hint: all three cases may be found in *The Adventures of Sherlock Holmes.*

26.     Which Scotland Yard inspector, who only worked with Sherlock on a single case, was originally from Scotland?

27.     What Scotland Yarder, "young and inexperienced," soon "changed his manner" when he learned that out of Sherlock's last fifty-three cases "the police had all the credit in forty-nine"?

28.     Upon his return to Baker Street after The Great Hiatus, Holmes chafed Lestrade by telling him "three undetected murders in one year won't do." On which case, however, did Holmes compliment Lestrade by saying that the detective handled it "fairly well"?

29.     Can you recall the name of the Yard's "Italian specialist" who aided Holmes in clearing up the mystery of the "Six Napoleons"?

30.     Can you name the Surrey Constabulary Inspector whose investigation into "The Adventure of Wisteria Lodge" might be looked upon as a rival to the Master's own work?

31.     Which inspector arrested the insidious Culverton Smith in "The Adventure of the Dying Detective"?

32. In addition to the Yard, Holmes occasionally worked with other law enforcement agencies. What was the name of Holmes's friend on the New York Police Bureau?

33. What was the name of Holmes's fellow detective on the Liverpool police force with whom he consulted in "The Adventure of the Cardboard Box"?

34. One of Holmes's "adversaries," in the words of the Master, "very nearly avenged Scotland Yard." Who or what received this dubious compliment from Sherlock?

35. Name the very first Scotland Yard inspector who Dr. Watson met after he and Holmes had moved into Baker Street.

36. Can you remember the name of the French detective who thought of Holmes as a "master" and who was busy translating some of his works into French?

37. Name the police constable who discovered the body of John Openshaw in the Thames.

38. Can you recall the one time when Sherlock refused to help the good Lestrade in any way?

# Answers

1.  Some nineteen different Scotland Yard inspectors are mentioned by name in the canon. (10)

2.  The name is Jones: Athelney and Peter. Though some believe that Athelney-Jones is a compound surname, that is not an opinion shared by this author. (2)

3.  Inspector Lestrade (1)

4.  Holmes and Lestrade collaborated on thirteen cases. (5)

5.  Inspector Gregson was Lestrade's chief competition. (1)

6.    Holmes only joined forces with Gregson on four cases. (3)

7.    *A Study in Scarlet* (1)

8.    "The Naval Treaty" (5)

9.    Lestrade's first initial was G. (1)

10.   Lestrade was a member of the Yard for forty years, from approximately 1862 to 1902. (2)

11.   Bow Street (2)

12.   Athelney Jones (2)

13.   John Rance (2)

14.   Constable MacPherson (2)

15.   Dr. Grimesby Roylott (2)

16.   Holmes expressed a special interest in the career of Stanley Hopkins. (1)

17.   "The Adventure of Black Peter" (2)

18.   "The Adventure of the Missing Three-Quarter" (2)

19.   Tobias (2)

20. The two divisions mentioned by their letters were the B and H divisions. (2—1 each)

21. The Norwood and Shadwell police stations are also mentioned. (2—1 each)

22. On a visit to the Scotland Yard Museum, you might see Von Herder's infamous air gun. (3)

23. Lestrade was retained by Miss Turner in "The Boscombe Valley Mystery." (2)

24. Hopkins consulted Holmes about the murders of Sir Eustace Brackenstall, Peter Carey and Willoughby Smith. (3—1 each)

25. Bradstreet and Holmes teamed up for "The Man with the Twisted Lip," "The Adventure of the Engineer's Thumb" and "The Adventure of the Blue Carbuncle." (6—2 each)

26. Alec MacDonald, with his hard Aberdonian accent, was originally from Scotland. (3)

27. Inspector Forbes (3)

28. Holmes complimented Lestrade on his handling of "The Molesay Mystery." (3)

29.  Inspector Hill was the Yard's Italian specialist. (5)

30.  Inspector Baynes's fine work on the case earned the Master's genuine respect. (2)

31.  Inspector Morton had the pleasure of arresting the villainous Smith. (2)

32.  Holmes's friend in New York was Wilson Hargreave. (2)

33.  Holmes contacted his friend Algar. (3)

34.  The *Cynea Capillata,* or "lion's mane," elicited that comment from Holmes. (2)

35.  Lestrade (1)

36.  Francois Le Villard (3)

37.  Police Constable Cook, of H Division (2)

38.  Lestrade was looking for two men who had burgled the home of Charles Augustus Milverton. Holmes refused his aid to Lestrade; otherwise, he would have been looking for Watson and himself. (3)

# Chapter 9
# Up and Down the Thames

1. London is a sprawling city. In which end of this great metropolis—east or west—would you find the docks and shipyards?

2. What establishment did Holmes describe to Watson as "the vilest murder trap on the whole riverside"?

3. Though ships figure in a great many of Sherlock's cases, only one is actually named after a ship. Which one is it?

4. Which of Holmes's many cases draws its title from the name of a sailor?

5. In *The Sign of Four,* where did Jonathan Small conceal his boat?

6.    What vessel was carrying John Douglas when he was apparently assassinated by members of the Moriarty gang?

7.    Many ships and shipping companies are mentioned throughout the canon. What is the full name of the shipping firm for which the murderous James Browner worked?

8.    What was the name of Peter Carey's vessel?

9.    What type of weapon was used to murder the aforementioned skipper?

10.   The River Police are more properly known as the Thames Division Scotland Yard. All told, they are involved in three of the Master's many cases. Which ones?

11.   Who was the captain of the *Lone Star,* and where was she bound on her final voyage?

12.   What was the only thing that could have identified Holmes's craft as a police launch in *The Sign of Four?*

13.   Watson returned from his service overseas aboard a British troopship. What was the name of this vessel, which brought the good doctor safely home to England?

14. Can you remember the name of the speedy launch hired by Jonathan Small that led Holmes and his friends on a merry chase down the Thames?

15. Which of the many vessels mentioned in the canon is referred to as a "Chin-China coaster"?

16. What was the name of the vessel on which the homicidal James Browner served as steward?

17. What was the name of the brig which picked up the survivors of the mutiny aboard the *Gloria Scott*?

18. Speaking of the *Gloria Scott*, what was the name of the man who led the mutiny aboard her?

19. Baron Gruner was planning to leave London aboard a ship owned by the Cunard Line. What was the name of the vessel which the Baron never made?

20. As long as we are talking about missing ships, what was the name of the ship on which Jonathan Small had planned to escape to Brazil, but which, because of Holmes, he never made?

21. Jack Croker, the killer of Sir Eustace Brackenstall, served on two ships that we

know of. Can you provide the names of both vessels? Bonus points if you can name his position on each.

22. What was the name of the ill-fated vessel that sank off the Portuguese coast with all the members of the Worthingdon bank gang aboard?

23. What were the names of the three sailors who visited Baker Street in connection with the case of "Black Peter"?

24. In the case of "The *Gloria Scott*," Trevor Senior lived to regret rescuing a young seaman, because when the sailor saw his savior years later, he began to blackmail him. What was the name of that nautical ne'er-do-well?

25. In his pockets Enoch Drebber carried two letters from a steamship line. With which company had Drebber been corresponding?

26. What is the name of the peninsula that juts out into the Thames? It is located near the West India docks, and Holmes and Watson pursued Jonathan Small's speedy craft around it.

27. Which section of the Thames is known as the furthest point up river for large sea-going vessels?

28. What was the name of the port in Cornwall from which the *Gloria Scott* embarked on her tragic final voyage?

29. In his disguise as Altamont, what was Holmes supposed to deliver to the German spymaster in "His Last Bow"?

30. What was the name of the steamship line that owned the *Rock of Gibraltar* and which Holmes visited in connection with "The Adventure of the Abbey Grange"?

31. "The Naval Treaty," which was stolen from Percy Phelps, had been drawn up between England and what other country?

32. What was the name of the sham chaplain aboard the *Gloria Scott* who helped to distribute pistols to the mutinous convicts?

33. In which adventure did Holmes's disguise as an asthmatic old master mariner prove so convincing that he deceived both Dr. Watson and an inspector from Scotland Yard?

34. Where did Holmes request that the police launch meet him prior to his voyage down the Thames in *The Sign of Four,* and what time did he want it there?

# Answers

1. Look for the docks in the East End. (1)

2. That distinction was earned by that infamous opium den, the Bar of Gold. (2)

3. "The *Gloria Scott*" (1)

4. "The Adventure of Black Peter" (1)

5. Small hid his launch in Jacobsen's Yard. (3)

6. Douglas had booked passage aboard the *Palmyra*. (3)

7. Browner was employed by the Liverpool, Dublin and London Steam Packet Co. (5)

# Up and Down the Thames—Answers

8.   Carey captained the *Sea Unicorn.* (3)

9.   Appropriately enough, Carey was killed with a harpoon. (2)

10.   The River Police figure in *The Sign of Four,* "The Five Orange Pips" and "The Adventure of the Cardboard Box." (3—1 each)

11.   Captained by James Calhoun, the *Lone Star* was bound for Savannah, Georgia, when she went down. (2—1 each)

12.   A green lantern (5)

13.   Watson was sent home on the *Orontes.* (3)

14.   Small hired the *Aurora.* (2)

15.   The *Gloria Scott* (3)

16.   Browner was a steward aboard the *May Day.* (3)

17.   The *Hotspur* (3)

18.   Jack Prendergast led the on-board insurrection. (3)

19.   Gruner had booked passage on the *Ruritania* prior to his unfortunate accident. (5)

Up and Down the Thames—Answers

20. Small had planned to sail to South America on board the *Esmerelda*. (5)

21. Aboard the *Rock of Gibraltar*, Croker was the first officer; for his fine work, he was named captain of the *Bass Rock*. (4—2 each; 4 bonus—2 each)

22. The *Norah Creina* (3)

23. James Lancaster, Hugh Pattins and Patrick Cairns (3—1 each)

24. Hudson (2)

25. The Guion Steamship Line (5)

26. The Isle of Dogs (4)

27. That section of the Thames is known as "The Pool." (4)

28. The ill-fated *Gloria Scott* set sail from Falmouth. (2)

29. Holmes, as Altamont, had promised to deliver naval signals. (2)

30. Holmes stopped in at the Adelaide-Southampton Line in Pall Mall. (3)

31. Italy (2)

32. Wilson was the rascal's name. (2)

33. *The Sign of Four* (1)

34. He asked that it be at the Westminster Steps at seven p.m. (5—4 for the location, 1 for the time)

# Chapter 10
# I Am the Last Court
# of Appeal

1.  Early on in his career Holmes knew that
    he had found his *méiter*. Which of his first
    cases prompted him to tell Watson that
    he was the "final court of appeal"?

2.  In which of his later cases did Holmes alter
    the wording if not the intent and refer to
    himself by the title of this chapter?

3.  Holmes quite often took the law into his
    own hands; in fact, he is on record as hav-
    ing committed no fewer than four acts of
    burglary. Name each man whose home
    was burgled by Holmes.

4.  Holmes was also not averse to the con-
    cept of private vengeance; in fact, he

vowed to avenge the death of John Openshaw. On whom did the Master plan on taking out his revenge?

5. Name the big-game hunter and African explorer who used the Devil's Foot root to murder Mortimer Tregennis and whom Holmes allowed to escape untouched by the law.

6. Holmes would not expose the murderer of Sir Eustace Brackenstall to prosecution. Whom did Holmes allow to escape from the clutches of the British legal system in that instance?

7. What was the name of the above character's chief confederate, whom Sherlock also shielded from the law?

8. Holmes had his feminine felon caught red-handed, but he permitted her to restore the document which she had pilfered before her husband found her out. Who is she?

9. Sherlck often looked the other way and thus, in a sense, condoned criminal action on the part of another. What was the name of the man who concealed his sister's death for a time by having a man masquerade as the dead woman?

10.   Holmes allowed this woman to pay five thousand pounds for a trip around the world for the victim's mother in lieu of punishing her. What is the name of *la belle dame sans merci*?

11.   Holmes would not expose the killer of Charles McCarthy provided that the accused was acquitted; in fact, Holmes told the killer, "It's not for me to judge you." Who was this murderer?

12.   Prior to Holmes's discovery, who was the only man in London who knew the man with the twisted lip's real identity?

13.   What character, whom the Master described as the perfect compound of "bully, coward and sneak," was allowed to get off scot-free in "Silver Blaze" despite the fact that he would have committed a felony but for Sherlock's intervention?

14.   Speaking of getting off scot-free, who was responsible for the death of John Straker and was excused by Holmes because he believed that the act had been committed in self-defense?

15.   Sherlock once claimed that he was "indirectly responsible" for the death of this individual; however, he added, "I cannot say that it is likely to weigh heavily upon

my conscience." Who was Sherlock's inadvertent victim?

16. The Master, "to avert scandal," allowed the duo responsible for the theft of and damage done to the beryl coronet to escape formal charges. What were their names?

17. Occasionally, Holmes's excursions outside the law involved Watson. In one case he asked Watson, "You don't mind breaking the law?" The good doctor was not averse, and his mission in that instance was to throw a "plumber's rocket" into a house as a diversion. Whose house was it?

18. Sherlock let the criminal responsible for the theft of the famous Blue Carbuncle escape punishment. At the same time he commented, "I am not retained by the police to supply their dificiencies." What was the name of that fortunate felon?

19. On one occasion Holmes wired Inspector Forbes after allowing a culprit to flee. Sherlock justified his action by explaining that the government "would very much rather the affair never got as far as a police court." Who was the thief, and what had he stolen?

20.     Holmes accused the Duke of Holdernesse
        of "condoning a felony"; then the Master
        compounded the injustice by allowing the
        instigator of the kidnapping of the Duke's
        son to escape unscathed. Whom did
        Holmes pardon, and why did he do it?

21.     In perparing to burgle the home of the
        "king of all the blackmailers," Holmes
        opined that his actions were "morally
        justifiable though technically criminal";
        however, a woman entered the room and
        murdered the man. Against whom did this
        unknown woman, whom Sherlock let
        flee, claim to be carrying incriminating
        documents?

22.     Together with Mr. Hilton Soames, Holmes
        and Watson once conducted "a small,
        private court-martial." At that proceeding,
        who was put on trial?

23.     Holmes once deceived a young woman
        in a telegraph office because he needed
        to see the "counterfoil" of a certain com-
        munique, the last words of which were
        "for God's sake." Who sent the telegraph
        which Holmes looked at illegally, and to
        whom was it addressed?

24.     Can you name the murderer who was
        unofficially tried with Holmes as judge and
        Watson as jury? He was acquitted with the

word *Vox populis, vox Die.* Hint: The same case caused Sherlock to remark, "I had rather play tricks with the law of England than with my conscience."

25.    "If the law can do nothing, we must take the risk ourselves," Holmes once remarked to Watson. Whom was Holmes preparing to rescue from the clutches of the Tiger of San Pedro when he made this remark?

26.    In point of fact, who actually saved the individual from the Tiger of San Pedro, though admittedly Holmes was responsible for the savior being in the right place at the right time?

27.    Holmes once forced his way into a house in order to search it. Before he could finish, however, the police arrived, and he was escorted out. Whose house had Holmes invaded without virtue of a warrant?

28.    Who or what was Sherlock hoping to find in that house?

29.    Among his other "illegal" activities, Holmes was once accused of kidnapping "a German subject," and he was indeed guilty. Who made the accusation which Holmes so blithely ignored?

30.     Who helped the Master in that particular breach of the law?

31.     Holmes was willing to "compound a felony" by letting Count Sylvius off the hook. What did the nobleman have to give the Master in return for his freedom?

32.     Although technically not a client, this woman sought out Holmes because she wanted to find "one man of judgment" to whom she could bare her soul. What was the name of this woman who held Holmes in such high regard?

33.     Sherlock must have been a bad influence on his fellow lodger, for in *The Hound of the Baskervilles* both Watson and Sir Henry were "aiding and abetting a felony." Whom were they shielding from the law?

34.     The Master once accused Watson of committing "libel" by calling this man a criminal. Whom was Holmes defending from Watson's slanderous attacks?

35.     Although he never touched the man, this individual was responsible for the death of Colonel James Barclay. Holmes let the secret of the Colonel's villany remain hidden and said nothing about the inadvertent tragedy. Who literally scared the Colonel to death?

36.    In Which case did the Master request that Watson join him at Goldini's and that the good doctor "bring a jemmy, dark lantern, chisel, and a revolver"?

# Answers

1.  Holmes made that remark in "The Musgrave Ritual." (5)

2.  The title of the chapter comes from a remark made by the Master in "The Five Orange Pips." (5)

3.  Holmes either burgled or attempted to burgle the homes of Hugo Oberstein, Baron Gruner, Charles Augustus Milverton and Josiah Amberley. (4—1 each)

4.  Captain James Calhoun of the *Lone Star* (2)

5.  Leon Sterndale (1)

6.   Jack Croker (1)

7.   Lady Mary Brackenstall, the former Mary Fraser (1)

8.   Lady Hilda Trelawney Hope (1)

9.   Sir Robert Norberton (1)

10.  Isadora Klein (1)

11.  John Turner (2)

12.  The lascar at the Bar of Gold (5)

13.  Silas Brown (3)

14.  Holmes concluded that Silver Blaze had in fact killed his trainer because the animal sensed that it was in danger. (1)

15.  Dr. Grimesby Roylott (2)

16.  Sir George Burnwell and Alice Holder (4—2 each)

17.  Irene Adler's house was the site of the rocket-throwing incident which caused Watson to cross over to the wrong side of the law. (3)

18.   James Ryder (2)

19.   Joseph Harrison had stolen the Naval Treaty. (4—2 each)

20.   Holmes excused the actions of James Wilder because the nobleman told Holmes that Wilder was his illegitimate son. (4—2 each)

21.   The unnamed woman claimed that she possessed letters that compromised the Countess d'Albert. (5)

22.   Bannister, the servant of Sir Jabez Gilchrist, was he party on trial. (3)

23.   Godfrey Staunton had sent the telegram, but, as Holmes learned from his "illegal" look at the counterfoil, Staunton had not written down the addressee's name. (4—2 each)

24.   Jack Croker (2)

25.   Miss Burnet, who was acting as governess to the deposed dictator's children and conspiring against the tyrant's life, was the cause of that remark. Her real name was Signora Victor Durando. (6—3 each)

26.   John Warner, former gardener at High Gables, actually rescued Miss Burnet. (10)

27. Holmes was searching the home of a man traveling under the name Dr. Henry Schlessinger. (2)

28. Sherlock was in search of Lady Frances Carfax. (2)

29. Von Bork (1)

30. Good old Watson was once again the Master's confederate in crime. (1)

31. Holmes asked the Count to surrender the Mazarin Stone. (1)

32. Eugenia Ronder (1)

33. They were guilty of not turning in Selden, the brother of Mrs. Barrymore. Selden had escaped from Princetown or Dartmoor Prison. (2)

34. Holmes said that Watson had libeled none other than Professor James Moriarty. (3)

35. Henry Woods (2)

36. "The Adventure of the Bruce-Partington Plans" (3)

# Chapter 11
# A Singular Set of People

1.      In the case of "The Naval Treaty," who was Percy Phelps's co-clerk who fell under suspicion of the theft because of his ethnic surname?

2.      What was the name of the *danseuse* at the Allegro who caused a scene at the wedding breakfast of Hatty Doran and Lord St. Simon?

3.      In addition to Jonathan Small, what were the names of the other members of the Sign of Four?

4.      Which of the Master's many clients came to see him wearing a mask so that no one, including Holmes, would recognize him?

# A Singular Set of People—Questions

5. What pseudonym did this client use in place of his own well-known name?

6. Hatty Doran had thought her husband dead, which was why she agreed to wed Lord St. Simon; however, in the church she saw that her first spouse was still very much alive, and so she bolted after the wedding. What was the name of Hatty's first husband?

7. What was the name of Jephro Rucastle's sadistic son who so enjoyed bashing cockroaches with a slipper—a fact whose significance was not lost on Holmes?

8. What was the alias used by John Straker while he was carrying on his illicit affair?

9. What was the name of the child that Mrs. Grant Munro had by her first husband, John Hebron?

10. Can you remember which character first suggested that Holmes should pursue a career as a detective?

11. What was the name of the butler at Hurlstone—a sort of local Don Juan— who was found dead in the cellar without the object of his desire?

12. What was the name of the man who Colonel Barclay "had betrayed into the hands of the Sikhs during the Mutiny"?

13. What was the name of the Baker Street boy who Holmes left watching this individual?

14. Name the man who was held prisoner in "The Greek Interpretor" with his face covered over with sticking plaster.

15. This character donned a dark beard and followed Violet Smith to and from the railway station each weekened on a bicycle. What was the name of this duplicitous protector?

16. Can you recall the name of the man who "knocked out" Holmes's left canine "in the waiting room of Charing Cross"?

17. What was the title of the Duke of Holdernesse's son who was kidnapped in "The Adventures of the Priory School"?

18. Who authored *Sidelights on Horace*, served as principal of the Priory School, and was responsible for bringing the case to Holmes's attention?

19. Finally, with regard to that particular case, what was the unfortunate German master's name who followed the Duke's son from the school and in doing so lost his life?

20.     A reporter by trade, this man awoke to find his bust of Napoleon gone, a dead body on his doorstep, and because of police interrogations, his scoop lost to all the competing papers. What was the name of this most unfortunate individual?

21.     This man was responsible for administering the Fortescue Scholarship at the College of St. Luke's. When the papers were pilfered, he applied to Holmes for help in avoiding a scandal. Who was he?

22.     What was the real Christian name of Professor Coram, who attempted to conceal his wife in a secret room after she had accidentally killed his scretary?

23.     What was the name of Godfréy Staunton's frugal uncle who Holmes apparently delighted in tweaking by indicating that the man might soon be robbed?

24.     Which of the foreign spies living in London led a double life on the continent?

25.     Name the man who, after dining with Aloysius Garcia, was awakened in the middle of the night and then awoke alone in the house of his host. As a result of his irregular adventure, Holmes became a figure in "The Adventure of Wisteria Lodge."

26.  What was the name of the dermatologist whom Holmes consulted in "The Adventure of the Blanched Soldier" and who diagnosed Godfrey Emsworth's condition as pseudo-leprosy?

27.  In "The Adventure of the Three Gables" Holmes consulted an individual whom he described affectionately as his "human reference book on scandal." What is the name of this knowledgeable individual?

28.  Can you call to mind the name of the woman of pure Spanish extraction who was painted as a villainess by Douglas Maberly and whom Holmes described using the title of a poem by Keats?

29.  What was the name of Sherlock's singular client whose many and varied interests included coins, fossils and insects, among other things, and who ended up in a nursing home when his dreams of wealth were shattered?

30.  What was the name of the man who impersonated Lady Beatrice Falder after she passed away? For a bonus, supply his wife's maiden name.

31.  Besides Jonathan Small, another of Holmes's clients had an artificial leg. A villain at heart, he came to the Master out

of "pure swank," and Holmes stated that the man was "headed more for Broadmoor than for the scaffold." Who was this rather unique personage?

32. What was the name of Bartholomew Sholto's porter, an ex-boxer with whom Holmes had once gone three rounds?

33. What was the name of Jonathan Small's diminutive but deadly companion?

34. For whom was Watson looking in the Bar of Gold when he discovered Holmes posing as an old opium addict?

35. Who was the young physician who authored a monograph upon "obscure nervous lesions," a work for which he won the Bruce Pinkerton Prize and which Dr. Watson had read?

36. This man, whom Watson described as "an Abraham Lincoln keyed to base uses instead of high ones," had served in the American Senate but was nevertheless rebuked by Holmes for his improper advances towards Grace Dunbar. Who was he?

37. Who was the young woman with whom Professor Presbury had became infatuated and to whom he was eventually engaged?

# Answers

1.  Charles Gorot (3)

2.  Flora Miller (2)

3.  Mahomet Singh, Dost Akbar and Abdullah Kahn (3—1 each)

4.  The King of Bohemia has that distinction. (1)

5.  His Highness introduced himself to Holmes as Count Von Kramm. (2)

6.  Francis Hay Moulton (3)

7.  Edward (2)

# A Singular Set of People—Answers

8.      Straker used the name Derbyshire. (3)

9.      Effie (1)

10.     Trevor Senior first suggested that Holmes pursue a career as a detective, and for that fortuitous remark we are all in his debt. (2)

11.     Richard Brunton (1)

12.     Henry Woods (1)

13.     Simpson (5)

14.     Paul Kratides (1)

15.     Bob Carruthers (1)

16.     Matthews (10)

17.     Lord Saltire (3)

18.     Thorneycroft Huxtable (1)

19.     Heidegger (3)

20.     Horace Harker (3)

21.     Hilton Soames (1)

22.     Sergius (3)

23.     Lord Mount James (5)

# A Singular Set of People—Answers

24.     Eduardo Lucas (2)

25.     Mr. John Scott Eccles (1)

26.     Sir James Saunders (5)

27.     Langdale Pike (5)

28.     Isadora Klein (2)

29.     Nathan Garrideb (2)

30.     Norlett impersonated Lady Beatrice; his wife Carrie worked as Lady Beatrice's maid using her maiden name, Evans. (5—3 for the bonus)

31.     Josiah Amberley (4)

32.     McMurdo (2)

33.     Tonga (2)

34.     Isa Whitney (2)

35.     Dr. Percy Trevelyan (2)

36.     J. Neil Gibson (1)

37.     Alice Morphy (5)

# Chapter 12
# Untold Tales

1.   At one point in his career, Holmes was summoned to Odessa to clear up a murder case. What name did Watson give to the affair?

2.   About the same time Holmes was responsible for "clearing up the singular tragedy" of a set of brothers at Trincomalee. What was the surname of those unfortunate siblings?

3.   Can you recollect the name of the couple whose "separation case" included the fact that the husband concluded each meal by "taking out his false teeth and hurling them at his wife"?

4.     An adventure alluded to by Watson in "The Five Orange Pips" concerned a group "who held a luxurious club in the lower vault of a furniture warehouse." What was the name of this group into whose affairs the Master took a look?

5.     Holmes once dealt with a case on "the island of Uffa." What was the name of the family involved in this "singular adventure"?

6.     Who was the client saved by Sherlock in the untold tale of the "Tankerville Club scandal"?

7.     Helen Stoner in "The Adventure of the Speckled Band" was recommended to Sherlock by a Mrs. Farintosh. Holmes, who recalled the case, said it was before Watson's time. The exploit centered around a piece of jewelry. What type of bauble brought Mrs. Farintosh to Baker Street?

8.     Just prior to "The Adventure of the Noble Bachelor" Holmes had been working on a case involving a furniture van. With what section of London was the van associated?

9.     Another of Sherlock's untold tales was a "singular affair" involving a crutch. Of what material was the crutch constructed?

10. Sherlock once handled a case involving a man with a clubfoot and "his abominable wife." What was the name of this doubly unfortunate couple?

11. In another case alluded to but never detailed, Holmes crossed paths with a man named Vanberry. All that we know about this mysterious figure is his occupation. What did the enigmatic Vanberry do for a living?

12. In "The Adventure of the Norwood Builder" Watson mentions a Dutch steamship which he claims almost cost him and Holmes their lives. Can you recall the name of this villainous vessel?

13. When Thorneycroft Huxtable burst into the Baker Street suite on May 16, he entreated Holmes to return with him to Mackleton. Holmes initially refused, citing two cases: one in which he had been retained and the other of which was coming up for trial. Can you remember them?

14. What was the name of the family whose "dreadful business" was first brought to Sherlock's "notice by the depth which the parsley had sunk into the butter on a hot day"?

15. What was the name of the "Boulevard assassin," whose tracking and arrest won

for the Master an autographed "letter of thanks from the French President and the Order of the Legion of Honour"?

16. In still another adventure about which we are in the dark, a man named Wilson was arrested. The only other fact that we know about him is his rather unusual occupation. What was it?

17. What two cases did the Master handle at the express request of His Holiness the Pope?

18. One of the Master's more promising unrelated narratives—at least from its description—involved a woman with no powder on her nose. Where did Holmes say this woman was from?

19. In the "bogus laundry affair" Holmes and Lestrade received aid from a certain "chap." Although we know nothing more about the case, we do know that helpful fellow's name. What is it?

20. In "The Disappearance of Lady Frances Carfax" Holmes initially planned to send Watson to France as his agent. Sherlock claimed that he could not leave London while an elderly client of his was "in such mortal terror of his life." Can you call to mind the name of that fearful client?

21.  Which ruler employed Holmes in a case that "called for immediate action as political consequences of the gravest kind might arise" and so delayed the Master's inquiry into "The Blanched Soldier"?

22.  What ship would we associate with "the giant rat of Sumatra," a tale, Watson cautions us, "for which the world is not yet prepared"?

23.  A "yeggman" is a slang term for a safecracker. Under Holmes' *V* entries, he had a case involving a "Yeggman" and a person whose surname began with the letter *V*. What was the individual in question's name?

24.  A number of the Master's cases ended in failure. One of those unfortunate exploits involved "a cutter . . . which sailed one morning into a small patch of mist from which she never again emerged nor was anything further ever heard of herself of her crew." What was the name of that ill-fated ship?

25.  Another of Sherlock's off-the-record failures involved Mr. James Philmore, who stepped back into his house one day to retrieve something and "was never more seen in this world." What was it that Philmore sought right before he vanished?

26.  Can you remember the name of the "well-known journalist and duellist who was found stark-staring mad with a matchbox in front of him which contained a remarkable worm said to be unknown to science"?

27.  Holmes initially put off entering the case of the "Retired Colourman" and sent Watson as his agent because he was right in the middle of a case revolving around a number of Coptic Patriarchs. Exactly how many religious men were involved?

28.  In addition to *The Sign of Four*, on what case did the Master work with Athelney Jones?

29.  What was the name of the woman whose husband Holmes easily located when the police had given him up for dead?

30.  Mycroft expected his brother to consult him in the "Manor House" case, but Sherlock was able to determine the culprit without recourse to his older sibling. What was the felon's name?

31.  Sherlock "defended the unfortunate Mme. Montpensier from the charge of murder which hung over her in connection with the 'death' of her stepdaughter . . . who was found six months later alive

and married in New York." What was the girl's name?

32. There was "a famous card scandal at the Norpareil Club" during which Holmes exposed this individual's "atrocious behaviour." What was the name of that card-playing scoundrel?

33. Sherlock once solved a poisoning case in which he "was able, by winding up the dead man's watch, to prove that it had been wound up two hours before"—a deduction which was of the utmost importance in clearing up the case. In which borough of London did the case take place?

34. At the beginning of "The Reigate Squires" Watson refers to one—or possibly two—untold tales. He alludes to the case of the Netherland-Sumatra Co. and the "colossal schemes" of a certain nobleman. What was the name of this pernicious peer?

35. Watson tells us that Violet Smith's visit in "The Solitary Cyclist" was "most unwelcome" to Holmes, for Sherlock was immersed in the "very abstruse and complicated problems concerning the peculiar persecution" to which a well-known tobacco millionaire had been subjected. What was that wealthy client's name?

36.    What was the name of the forger whom Holmes and Watson captured near Farnham on the borders of Surrey but about whose case Watson says nothing more?

37.    Mrs. Warren brought "The Adventure of the Red Circle" to Sherlock's attention because she was concerned about the mysterious lodger she had just taken in. However, the principal reason she sought out Sherlock was because he had helped another of her tenants. Who was the first boarder helped by Holmes?

# Answers

1.  Watson called that particular affair the case of the Trepoff murder. (3)

2.  Atkinson (3)

3.  That unhappy couple was named Dundas. (3)

4.  The Amateur Mendicant Society (1)

5.  The Grice Patersons (3)

6.  Major Prendergast (3)

7.  Holmes had been involved with a case that concerned an opal tiara. (2)

8.      Grosvenor Square (2)

9.      The crutch was made of aluminum. (1)

10.     Ricoletti (3)

11.     All we can say for certain about Vanberry is that he was a wine merchant. (3)

12.     The *Freisland.* (5)

13.     At the time Holmes was preoccupied with "the case of the Ferrers Documents and the Abergavenny murder." (4—2 each)

14.     Abernetty was the name of that unfortunate family. (2)

15.     Huret was the name of the infamous "Boulevard assassin." (4)

16.     Wilson was a "canary trainer." (2)

17.     On behalf of His Holiness, Holmes became involved with "the death of Cardinal Tosca" and "the case of the Vatican Cameos." (4—2 each)

18.     The woman sans make-up hailed from Margate. (3)

19.     Alridge is the name of the man who came to Holmes's aid. (5)

20.  Abrahams (2)

21.  In that particular case Holmes was working on behalf of the Sultan of Turkey. (3)

22.  The *Matilda Briggs* (2)

23.  Vanderbilt (2)

24.  The *Alicia* (3)

25.  Philmore stepped back into his home to retrieve his umbrella. (2)

26.  Isadora Persano (3)

27.  Two (1)

28.  Holmes and Athelney Jones joined forces on the Bishopgate Jewel case. (3)

29.  Mrs. Etherege (3)

30.  Adams (5)

31.  Mlle. Carere (3)

32.  The rascal's name was Colonel Upwood. (3)

33.  That particular poisoning case took place in Camberwell. (2)

34. What nefarious nobleman was none other than Baron Maupertuis. (3)

35. The name of Holmes's wealthy client was John Vincent Harden. (1)

36. Archie Stamford—presumably he is no relation to "young Stamford," who introduced Holmes and Watson (1)

37. Mr. Fairdale Hobbs (2)

# Chapter 13
# I Hear of Sherlock Everywhere

1.    Who uttered the words that make up the title of this chapter, and in what case were they said?

2.    Exactly how many place names are mentioned in the various titles of the canon? Do not count adjectives such as *Greek* when you arrive at your total unless the adjective names a specific place.

3.    Charles McCarthy's farm had the same name as one of Sherlock's clients. What was the name of the blackmailer McCarthy's estate in Boscombe Valley?

4.    Can you recall the name of the estate inhabited by that old Saxon family the Roylotts?

5.  Alexander Holder took the beryl coronet—a national treasure—home with him in the evening. What was the name of the house from which the priceless artifact was stolen?

6.  Hurlstone is located in western Sussex. Obviously the Master's reputation had spread that far, but can you recall the name of Holmes's client who lived in the manor house at Hurlstone?

7.  At the beginning of "The Reigate Squires," Holmes had fallen ill in a hotel in a city on the continent. What was the name of the hotel and the city?

8.  Can you recall the name of Colonel Barclay's villa in Aldershot which Holmes visited in connection with "The Crooked Man"?

9.  What was the name of Harold Latimer's rented house in Beckenham? Holmes received a message from one J. Davenport informing him that Sophy Kratides was living there "at present."

10. Not only was Holmes well known in England, but as we have seen he had also attained a degree of international celebrity. Can you recall the investigation in which Holmes demonstrated "the true facts of

the case to Monsieur Dubuque of the Paris police and Fritz von Waldheim, the well-known specialist of Danzig—both of whom had wasted their energies upon what proved to be side-issues"?

11. Whom did Holmes visit at Khartoum during The Great Hiatus—presumably under the name of Sigerson but perhaps under his own well-known name?

12. What was the name of the house which Jonas Oldacre had built and in which Holmes discovered him hiding?

13. Holmes once sent a message to Elrige's Farm, East Ruston, while he was in that area working on a case. Who came in reply to Sherlock's summons?

14. On one occasion the Master was summoned to Norfolk by Mr. Hilton Cubitt. What was the name of Cubitt's eastern English estate?

15. What was the name of Bob Carruthers's home in Farnham to which he brought Violet Smith in "The Adventure of the Solitary Cyclist"?

16. In connection with which case do we hear of Sherlock toiling in Mackleton, and in what county might we look to find that fictitious city?

17. Holmes was asked to look into the tragedy at "Woodman's Lee." What is the popular epithet ascribed to that unfortunate occurrence?

18. Though hardly a client, this venal individual lived in Appledore Towers in Hampstead. What was the name of "the worst man in London," who lived there?

19. Holmes visited Kent on more than one occasion, but so far as we know he only visited the home of Professor Coram once. What was the name of the Professor's estate?

20. During his sojourn in England, the Tiger of San Pedro resided in "a famous old Jacobean grange." What was the name of the home to which Holmes tracked the Tiger?

21. We all know that Mr. John Scott Eccles was familiar with Holmes because Eccles came directly to Baker Street after spending a night in Wisteria Lodge. In what county is that home, and who was Eccles's host?

22. In addition to gaining a reputation, Holmes kept abreast of his competitors' reknown. With what mystery should we associate Mr. Leverton of Pinkerton's,

whom the Master met while tracing "The Red Circle"?

23. Holmes, as we discussed earlier, attempted to burgle the residence of Baron Gruner in Kensington. What was the name of the nobleman's estate?

24. In the case of "The Blanched Soldier" Holmes visited the residence of Colonel Emsworth in an effort to locate the Colonel's son, Godfrey. What was the name of the Emsworth estate?

25. Can you remember who resided in The Three Gables, and where in Middlesex that fine old home might be found?

26. Perhaps the most singular name of any residence in the canon was that of the home owned by Mr. Robert Ferguson in Sussex. Can you recall the name of his handsome home?

27. Josiah Amberley's dwelling in Lewisham and the Bellamys' home in Fulworth shared a common appellation. By what name were both homes called?

28. What was the name of Bartholomew Sholto's residence in Upper Norwood?

29. What was the name of Mr. Frankland's— Sir Henry Baskerville's contumacious

neighbor—home in *The Hound of the Baskervilles*?

30. In what southwestern county might we find Baskerville Hall, Dartmoor and King's Pyland Stables?

31. What was the name of the house which Roaring Jack Woodley and the defrocked clergyman, Williamson, had leased in Farnham and to which they took Violet Smith after they kidnapped her?

32. Here's a real toughie! In which of Holmes's cases did the Master comment, "We have touched on three English counties in our short drive"?

33. In what number Lauriston Gardens was the body of Enoch Drebber discovered?

34. Who sent an urgent request for Holmes to come with all possible dispatch to Briarbrae, Woking?

35. Finally, where was the body of Aloysius Garcia found in "The Adventure of Wisteria Lodge"?

# Answers

1.  Mycroft made the statement in "The Greek Interpretor" by way of paying Watson a compliment as his brother's chronicler. (2—1 each)

2.  The answer is either fourteen or fifteen, depending upon whether or not you considered the *Gloria Scott*. The other places are Bohemia, Boscombe Valley, Copper Beeches, Reigate, Empty House, Norwood, Priory School, Abbey Grange, *The Valley of Fear*, Wisteria Lodge, Three Gables, Sussex, Thor Bridge and Shoscombe Old Place. (5)

3.  Hatherley (2)

4.    Stoke Moran (1)

5.    Holder's home was named Fairbank. (3)

6.    Reginald Musgrave, who knew Holmes in college, made his home at Hurlstone. (2)

7.    Watson was summoned to the Hotel Dulong in Lyons. (4—2 each)

8.    Barclay's villa was named Lachine. (3)

9.    Latimer had rented The Myrtles. (3)

10.   Watson informs us that this encounter took place in connection with "The Adventure of the Second Stain." However, this seems not to be the case unless Watson, for state reasons, cut his narrative short in the canon. (3)

11.   The Khalifa (5)

12.   Oldacre's estate was Deep Dene House. (3)

13.   Holmes expected Abe Slaney, "the most dangerous crook in Chicago," to respond, and indeed Slaney did come directly. (2)

14.   Cubitt lived at Ridling Thorpe Manor, which in some editions appears as Riding Thorpe Manor. (3)

15.     Chiltern Grange (3)

16.     "The Adventure of the Priory School"
        brought the Master to Mackleton, which
        is located in Hallamshire. (4—2 each)

17.     "The Adventure of Black Peter" (1)

18.     Charles Augustus Milverton (2)

19.     Yoxley Old Place was the name of the
        Professor's estate. (3)

20.     The Tiger of San Pedro was hiding out in
        a house named High Gable. (3)

21.     Wisteria Lodge is located near Esher, and
        Aloysius Garcia was the host of Mr. Ec-
        cles. (4—2 each)

22.     "The Long Island Cave Mystery" (5)

23.     Gruner resided at Vernon Lodge. (3)

24.     The Emsworths lived at Tuxbury Old Park.
        (2)

25.     Mrs. Mary Maberley lived in The Three
        Gables, which is a house in Harrow
        Weald. (2—1 each)

26.     Ferguson lived at Cheeseman's Lamberley
        in Sussex. (3)

27. Both homes were called The Haven. (2)

28. Pondicherry Lodge (1)

29. Lafter Hall (5)

30. Devonshire, or Devon (1)

31. Charlington Hall (3)

32. "The Man with the Twisted Lip" caused the Master to make the remark, and the three counties were Middlesex, Surrey and Kent. (5)

33. Drebber's body was found in 3 Lauriston Gardens. (1)

34. Percy Phelps (2)

35. Garcia's body was discovered on Oxshott Common. (4)

# Chapter 14
# Villains and Blackguards

1.  This villain had pierced ears and an acid stain on his face, as well as an education from Eton and Oxford. Holmes considered him "the fourth smartest man in London and the third most daring." Who is he?

2.  This ne'er-do-well had murdered one of his nieces and was nightly attempting to do away with her twin sister. What was the name of this cowardly killer?

3.  Can you recall the name of the man who tried to take the life of Victor Hatherley but only succeeded in severing the engineer's thumb?

4.     This rogue kept his daughter prisoner to prevent her marriage to Mr. Fowler. He also arranged for a woman to impersonate his child and thus discourage her suitor. What was the name of this fraudulent father?

5.     What was the real name of the brothers, one of whom decoyed Hall Pycroft to Birmingham while the other took his place as a clerk at Mawson and Williams?

6.     The Cunninghams of Reigate were being blackmailed by their coachman; when they murdered him, Holmes became involved. What was the name of their unscrupulous servant?

7.     What was the real name of Blessington, who had become Dr. Percy Trevelyan's resident patient?

8.     If you came up with the answer to the previous question, you should know that the man was a member of a famous, or perhaps infamous is more appropriate, gang. What was the name of that troupe of thieves? Can you name his four accomplices?

9.     The Master was unable to save Paul Kratides, but he believed that Sophy Kratides eventually stabbed the two men

who had kidnapped her and tortured her brother. What were their names?

10. In his futile attempt to recover the Naval Treaty, which he had stolen, the thief flew at Holmes with a knife and cut him on the hand before Holmes subdued him. Who was this murderous traitor?

11. Can you recollect the name of the bullying thief with whom Holmes engaged in a short boxing match in a public house near Farnham?

12. In "The Adventure of the Priory School" a German master was murdered. What was the killer's name?

13. Whom did Holmes tell Watson—after the demise of Moriarty, of course—was the "worst man in London"?

14. Can you call to mind the name of the Italian workman who stole the pearl of the Borgias and concealed it in a bust of Napoleon?

15. Speaking of that particular tale, in "The Six Napoleons" we are told that "one of the greatest cut-throats in London" was an Italian from Naples. This individual was stabbed to death by the man who had stolen the Borgia pearl. What was the cut-throat's name?

16. Who was the student whom Holmes correctly collared for cheating in "The Adventure of the Three Students"?

17. Whom did Sherlock suspect that vengeance had caught up with when he read about the deaths of the Marquese of Montalva and Signor Rulli, his secretary?

18. What was Giuseppe Gorgiano, sometimes known as "Black Gorgiano," known as in the south of Italy?

19. Whom did the Master trap with a phony newspaper ad in "The Adventure of the Bruce-Partington Plans"?

20. What was the real name of the knave who had a jagged left ear and who used the name Dr. Schlessinger in his encounter with the Master?

21. This killer stole *radix pedis diaboli* and used it on his siblings. His two brothers went insane and his sister died. He later suffered a similar fate in a wonderful example of poetic justice. Can you name the two killers in this tale?

22. What was the name of the Prussian spy master who recruited Holmes in his guise as Altamont?

23.   Holmes always showed a healthy respect for a worthy opponent. What was the name of "the Austrian murderer" about whom Sherlock suggested, "There is no more dangerous man in Europe"?

24.   Can you remember the names of the two pugilists employed by lawbreakers who visited Baker Street in totally unrelated cases?

25.   Here's a toughie: What was the name of the youngest wrong-doer Holmes encountered, if not in his career, at least in the canon?

26.   Eugenia Ronder did away with her husband at Abbas Parva. Can you recall the name of the strong man who conspired with her against her spouse?

27.   Roger Baskerville masqueraded as a schoolmaster in England for a time before he started to call himself Stapleton. What name did he use while holding classes?

28.   What was the name of the Notting Hill murderer who met the death designed for Sir Henry?

29.   What was the title given to Jack McGinty in his lodge at Vermissa Valley?

30. By what name were the Ancient Order of Freemen commonly known?

31. What were the real names of the men who presented themselves to Victor Hatherley as Colonel Lysander Stark and his secretary, Mr. Ferguson?

32. Originally who was suspected of murdering Sir Eustace Brackenstall, a belief which, though totally erroneous, Holmes did nothing to discourage after he had learned the truth?

33. What name was the Tiger of San Pedro traveling under while he was in England?

34. Steve Dixie took his orders from Barney Stockdale. Who gave Stockdale his orders?

35. Who was responsible for killing Hilton Cubitt in his home and driving Cubitt's wife to attempt suicide?

36. What was the name of the Duke of Holdernesse's illegitimate son who was responsible for kidnapping the Duke's legitimate son and rightful heir?

37. Who did Roaring Jack Woodley enlist to aid him in his plan to marry Violet Smith?

# Answers

1.     John Clay merited that comment from the Master. (1)

2.     Dr. Grimesby Roylott (1)

3.     Colonel Lysander Stark (2)

4.     Jephro Rucastle (1)

5.     Beddington (3)

6.     William Kirwan (5)

7.     Sutton (3)

8.     The Worthingdon bank gang, whose other members were Cartwright, who was hanged, Biddle, Hayward and Moffat.

Villains and Blackguards—Answers

(6—2 for the gang, 1 each for the members)

9. Harold Latimer and Wilson Kemp (2—1 each)

10. Joseph Harrison (1)

11. Holmes gave a short boxing lesson to Roaring Jack Woodley in a country pub in Farnham. (1)

12. Reuben Hayes was responsible for the death of Heidegger, the German master. (2)

13. Charles Augustus Milverton earned that distinction. (2)

14. Beppo (2)

15. Pietro Venucci (5)

16. Young Gilchrist (1)

17. When Holmes saw the newspaper report, he suspected that Juan Murillo, the Tiger of San Pedro, and Lucas, his secretary, had been assassinated. (2—1 each)

18. Gorgiano's nickname in southern Italy was "Death." (5)

19. Actually, Holmes snared two people. First, he trapped Colonel Valentine Walter, who

144

had actually stolen the plans; then, by means of a second ad, he trapped Hugo Oberstein, the agent to whom Walter had passed along the plans. (4—2 each)

20. Henry Peters (1)

21. Mortimer Tregennis drove his brothers insane and was responsible for the death of his sister; to avenge the death of the woman he loved, Leon Sterndale subjected Mortimer to the same Devil's Foot root. (2—1 each)

22. Von Bork (1)

23. Baron Adelbert Gruner (3)

24. Sam Merton and Steve Dixie (2—1 each)

25. That distinction would seem to belong to Jack Ferguson, who at age fifteen was trying to murder his infant stepbrother. (5)

26. Leonardo (3)

27. Vandeleur (5)

28. Selden (1)

29. McGinty was called the Bodymaster. (2)

30. The Freemen had become known as the Scowrers. (1)

31.    Stark's real name was Fritz, while Ferguson's was Dr. Becher. (4—2 each)

32.    The death of Sir Eustace Brackenstall was attributed to the Randalls, the Lewisham gang of burglars. (5)

33.    Henderson (3)

34.    Spencer John was Barney Stockdale's immediate superior and the leader of the gang. (5)

35.    Abe Slaney (3)

36.    James Wilder (2)

37.    A defrocked clergyman named Williamson (3)

# Chapter 15
# Singular Cases with a
# Numerical Bent

1.  A good many of the Master's cases had their commencement in the sitting room at Baker Street. How many stairs did a visitor have to climb to reach the flat shared by Holmes and Watson?

2.  Excluding adjectives like *final* and *solitary*, how many of the sixty cases in the canon contain numbers in their titles?

3.  Here's a real test of your powers of recall. What was the number of the cab in which Stapleton shadowed Henry Baskerville and Dr. Mortimer in London?

4.  What is the numerical countersign to "Nine to seven"?

5. How many different types of tire impressions did Sherlock claim familiarity with in "The Adventure of the Priory School"?

6. Holmes left a letter for Watson at the Reichenbach Falls. How many pages long was the Master's "final" epistle?

7. How many branches did the Franco-Midland Hardware Co., Ltd., have when Mr. Hall Pycroft was hired?

8. What train did Violet Smith take to London every weekend—except the last one, a fact for which Holmes did not allow?

9. How much did the Master have to pay to obtain the bust of Napoleon containing "the black pearl of the Borgias"?

10. What were the original odds on Silver Blaze to win the Wessex Cup?

11. Exactly how tall was the elm tree which played such a crucial role in the solution of "The Musgrave Ritual"? For a bonus, see if you can remember the tree's girth as well.

12. All told, how many orange pips were sent to the Openshaw family in "The Five Orange Pips"?

13. How many of Von Bork's best agents had ended up in prison due to Holmes's efforts while posing as Altamont?

14. What was the number of the page that Mrs. Maberley rescued from her son Douglas's *roman a clef*?

15. The first note left for John Ferrier by the Danite Band told him he had how many days left?

16. In the coded letter Trevor Senior received, he was to count only every certain word and omit the intervening ones. What was the key to this rather simplistic cipher?

17. Can you recall the date of the manuscript from Sir Charles Baskerville which Dr. Mortimer showed to Holmes while informing Sherlock about the legend?

18. What was the number of "broken threads" with which Holmes wound up at the start of *The Hound of the Baskervilles*?

19. This one's a little more difficult. How many "separate articles" were there in "The Naval Treaty," which Percy Phelps was entrusted with copying over?

20. In addition to Trevor Senior, how many

other convicts were aboard the *Gloria Scott* bound for Australia?

21. Holmes claimed to detect a number of "similarities of hand" in the handwriting of Old Cunningham and his son, Alec. Exactly how many likenesses was the Master able to ascertain?

22. A stoic by nature, Holmes abstained from food and water for how many days in order to deceive the wary Culverton Smith?

23. What is the number that most frequently appears in the various titles of Watson's narratives?

24. Holmes discovered an imprint in the garden outside of Wisteria Lodge. What size was the shoe that had made the imprint?

25. How much did Charles Augustus Milverton demand from Holmes's client Lady Eva Blackwell? Come up with the amount of Holmes's counteroffer, which Milverton refused, and you'll get a bonus.

26. In "The Adventure of the Bruce-Partington Plans," exactly how many papers were taken from the arsenal at Woolwich, and how many were found on the dead body of Cadogan West?

27.    Sir James Damery in "The Adventure of the Illustrious Client" gave Holmes his private phone number. It began with the letters XX. With what two digits did it conclude?

28.    In "The Stock-Broker's Clerk" Arthur Pinner quizzed Hall Pycroft about a number of stocks. How many stocks did Pinner inquire about? For a bonus, name the stocks.

29.    Holmes once told Watson, "When Moriarty goes, it will clear up over _____ mysteries." How many puzzles did Sherlock predict would be solved by the Professor's incarceration?

30.    What was the number of "separate ciphers" that Holmes claimed to have analyzed in "a trifling monograph upon the subject of secret writings" in "The Adventure of the Dancing Men"?

31.    Holmes detected a recurring pattern in the attacks of Professor Presbury's dog. How many days elapsed between the Professor's injections and the unfortunate hound's attacks?

32.    Holmes was able to trip up Josiah Amberley because the blackguard had lied

to him, claiming he had purchased two theater tickets when, in fact, he had only bought one. The row was B. What was the number of the single seat which the thrifty Amberley actually had purchased?

33.   How many shipyards did Holmes search prior to discovering the *Aurora* at Jacobsen's?

34.   How many different types of perfume did Sherlock tell Watson a criminal expert "must know" in *The Hound of the Baskervilles*?

35.   What was the first number of the coded message that Holmes received from Porlock, Moriarty's suborned associate?

36.   Can you remember the number of the lodge of the Ancient Order of Freemen in Vermissa Valley?

37.   If you knew the last question, this one should be a snap. What was the number of the lodge of the Ancient Order of Freemen that John McMurdo claimed to have joined in Chicago?

38.   What number did the Master trick Old Cunningham into writing on a piece of paper so that he could compare it with the portion of the note found in William Kirwin's hand?

# Answers

1. There were seventeen steps. (1)

2. Eight cases contain numbers in their titles. (2)

3. 2704 (10)

4. The proper response to "Nine to Seven" was "Seven to Five." (2)

5. Holmes claimed to be familiar with forty-two different types of tire impressions. (3)

6. Holmes's "last" letter was three pages long. (1)

7. 134 (5)

8. She caught the 12:22 as a rule. (2)

9. Holmes paid ten pounds. (2)

10. Silver Blaze was originally a 3:1 favorite. (2)

11. The tree in question was sixty-four feet high with a girth of twenty-three feet (3—and 2 for the bonus)

12. The Openshaw family received a total of fifteen pips. (3)

13. Five (1)

14. She saved page number 245. (5)

15. Ferrier was told that he had but twenty-nine days. (2)

16. He was to count every third word. (1)

17. 1742 (2)

18. Holmes wound up with three broken threads. (2)

19. The treaty contained twenty-six "separate articles." (3)

20. There were thirty-seven other convicts on board. (3)

21. Holmes mentioned the t's and e's and detected twenty-three other similarities, for a total of twenty-five. (5)

22. Holmes touched neither food nor water for three days. (1)

23. Three is the most common number, appearing in four different titles. (1)

24. Twelve (3)

25. Milverton demanded seven thousand pounds; Holmes offered two thousand. (3—2 for the bonus)

26. Ten papers were stolen but only seven were immediately recovered. (2—1 each)

27. 31 (5)

28. Pinner asked Pycroft about three stocks: Ayrshires, New Zealand Consolidated, and British Broken Hills. (2—give yourself 1 bonus for each stock you named)

29. Forty cases would be solved when Moriarty fell, according to Sherlock. (5)

30. Holmes claimed to have analyzed 160 ciphers. (2)

31. The attacks occurred every nine days. (1)

32. Amberley bought seat number B31. (3)

33. Holmes searched fifteen shipyards before he came to Jacobsen's. (2)

34. Seventy-five (2)

35. 534 (3)

36. 341 (1)

37. 29 (3)

38. Twelve (1)

# Chapter 16
# Something New Under the Sun

*The Strand Magazine*

"HE CURLED HIMSELF UP IN HIS
CHAIR."

1. This illustration originally appeared in the *Strand Magazine*. What is the name of the masterful illustrator whose work has become the standard by which all later Holmesian artists have had their renditions judged?

Granada Television

2.  Although Jeremy Brett, pictured above, is the most prominent of the recent Sherlockian impersonators, he is but the last in a series of many. Can you name the actor whom many consider to be the first great Sherlock?

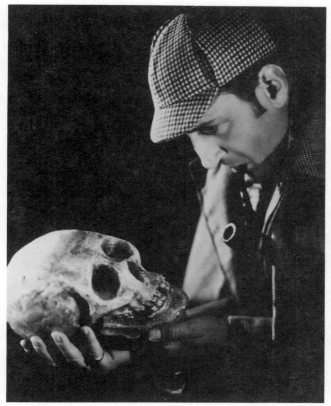

20th Century-Fox Film Corporation

3.     Basil Rathbone was easily the most
       publicized Holmes, yet he was far from the
       most prolific. Can you name the silent film
       star who appeared as the Master in forty-
       seven different films?

159

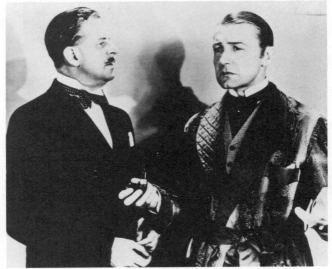

A Fox Film

4. The actor on the left, here playing Watson, a year later played Holmes in a remake of *A Study in Scarlet*. So far as we know, he is the only individual ever to have played both Holmes and Watson in films. Who is he?

A Fox Film

5.  Pictured above is the first actor whose Holmes died on screen. In a salute entitled *Paramount on Parade*, Paramount Studios inserted a Holmes sketch in which the diabolical Fu Manchu killed the Master. What was the actor's name who made the immortal Holmes mortal?

20th Century-Fox Film Corporation

6.  Two studios, 20th Century Fox Film Corporation and Universal Pictures, produced Holmes pictures starring Basil Rathbone and Nigel Bruce; however, there is a significant difference between the products of the two studios. What is it?

7.  Exactly how many films were made in which Rathbone played Holmes and Bruce appeared as Watson?

20th Century-Fox Film Corporation

8.   Certainly no true Holmes fan could have
     forgotten the name of the dog without
     whose aid Rathbone's *Hound of the
     Baskervilles* could never have been made.
     What was the real-life name of the film's
     title character?

9.    Pictured above are George Zucco, holding the pipe, and Henry Daniell, holding the gun. Both played the evil Professor Moriarty in other Rathbone films. Can you name the third actor who brought the Professor to life to antagonize Rathbone's Sherlock?

20th Century-Fox Film Corporation

10. Early films generally downplayed Holmes's predeliction for cocaine in a seven-percent solution. Still, one of Rathbone's films concludes with this telling line, "Oh, Watson! The needle!" Which film was it?

Universal Pictures

11.   In *Pursuit to Algiers* the action takes place
      aboard ship. The vessel's name is a
      canonical one. Can you remember it?

Universal Pictures

12.    In *Sherlock Holmes in Washington* Basil
       Rathbone as the Master searches for a
       piece of microfilm concealed in a match-
       book. What was the single letter which
       prominently adorned the face of that
       matchbook?

Universal Pictures

13.    In the film *Spider Woman* Holmes uses
       an alias in an attempt to win the con-
       fidence of the *femme fatale*. What was the
       name Sherlock used to try to deceive the
       Spider Woman?

14.    The actress above, who played the Spider
       Woman, holds an important place in the
       history of film, for she was the first woman
       ever to receive an Oscar for Best Support-
       ing Actress. Can you come up with her
       name and the film for which she received
       her award? Hint: It wasn't this one.

Universal Pictures

15.   Can you recall the name of the fraternal group who inhabited the *House of Fear*?

16. Above is a scene from the movie which concludes with Watson turning the tables and exclaiming, "Elementary, my dear Holmes! Elementary!" What film gave the good doctor the last laugh?

Universal Pictures

17. In the center is the fine character actor who played Inspector Lestrade in a number of Rathbone films. Can you recall his name?

Universal Pictures

18. In one of the Rathbone films we see Nigel Bruce as Watson reading one of his own stories in the latest issue of the *Strand Magazine.* In which movie did the scene occur, and which story from the canon was Watson reading aloud?

Universal Pictures

19. Can you recall both the actor on the left's name and the role he played in *The Pearl of Death*?

20.     The actor above is Paxton Whitehead,
        who was a hit as Holmes on Broadway.
        Can you recall the rather chilling title of
        the play?

Constantin-Film (Germany)

21.   Christopher Lee, pictured above, has had
      a long association with the canon. In ad-
      dition to playing the Master in a German
      film entitled *Sherlock Holmes and the
      Necklace of Death,* Lee has also been
      seen in English films as two other
      canonical figures. Whom did he play, and
      what were the films?

A Compton-Tekli-Sir Nigel Films Production
(British; U.S. release: Columbia Pictures)

22.     Name the film that featured John Neville
        as Holmes and Frank Finlay as Watson.

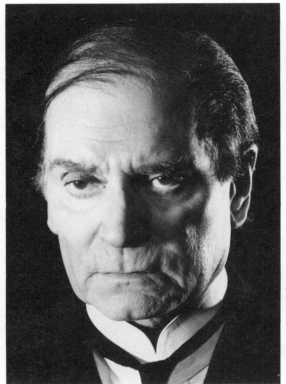

United Artists

23.    Nicholas Meyer wrote *The Seven-Per-Cent Solution* and later the screenplay for the film of the same title. What other Sherlockian pastiche—unfortunately, not yet made into a film—did Meyer author?

24.    Pictured above is the villainous Professor Moriarty in *The Seven-Per-Cent Solution*. Can you see beneath the make-up and recognize the actor who turned in that peerless performance?

20th Century-Fox Film Corporation

25.  In a rather unusual group shot we see John Huston as Moriarty, Charlotte Rampling as Irene Adler, Patrick MacNee as Watson, and Roger Moore as Holmes. What was the name of the two-hour telefilm with this inordinately talented cast?

26.    The exploits of Holmes have been seen
       on the big and little screens as well as on
       stage; however, only once have they been
       set to music. What was the name of the
       play, and who was the actor, pictured
       above, who played Holmes? For a bonus,
       name the actress.

20th Century-Fox Film Corporation

27. In *Sherlock Holmes's Smarter Brother,* the Master was not the focal point of the film. Pictured above is the actor who played Sherlock in that film. He also played Holmes for the BBC. What is his name?

28. Do you know the name of the character played by Gene Wilder in *Sherlock Holmes's Smarter Brother?*

The Mirsch Production Company

29. In *The Private Life of Sherlock Holmes* director Billy Wilder gave us two new faces as our old friends Holmes and Watson. Can you recall the actors' names?

British-Canadian film production

30.  Pictured above are James Mason as Watson and Christopher Plummer as Holmes. What was the name of the film in which they scowered London in search of Jack the Ripper?

Universal Pictures

31.   In 1972 Stewart Granger donned the
      deerstalker for a television version of *The
      Hound of the Baskervilles.* Can you recall
      the actor who boldly played the evil
      Stapleton as no man had ever played him
      before?

Courtesy of Granada Television

32.    Pictured above are Jeremy Brett as
       Holmes and Edward Hardwicke as Wat-
       son. Can you name the actor who
       preceeded Hardwicke as "Good Old
       Watson"?

Courtesy of Granada Television

33.     Here again is Jeremy Brett as the Master
        confronting the malignant Professor
        Moriarty at Reichenbach Falls. Who
        brought the Professor to life for the
        Grenada series?

Paul B. Goode

34.   To help celebrate Sherlock's one-hundredth anniversary, Broadway offered Frank Langella as the inimitable Holmes in a new play entitled *Sherlock's Last Case.* Who wrote it?

# Answers

1.  Sidney Paget (1)

2.  William Gillette (2)

3.  Eille Norwood (5)

4.  Reginald Owen (5)

5.  Clive Brook (3)

6.  20th Century Fox set their films in Holmes's own time—the Victorian era while Universal made the Master a contemporary figure circa 1940. (4)

7.  Rathbone and Bruce made fourteen films together: two for 20th Century Fox and twelve for Universal. (5)

8.   The Hound's name was Chief. (10)

9.   Lionel Atwill, who also appeared as Dr. Mortimer in *The Hound of the Baskervilles* (5)

10.  *The Hound of the Baskervilles* (3)

11.  Holmes booked passage aboard the S.S. *Friesland.* (3)

12.  The letter V (2)

13.  Raj ni Singh (2)

14.  Gail Sondergaard won the Oscar for her efforts in the 1936 film *Anthony Adverse.* (2)

15.  The Good Comrades (3)

16.  *The Adventures of Sherlock Holmes* (3)

17.  Dennis Hoey was the memorable Lestrade. (1)

18.  In *Dressed to Kill* Watson read a short passage from "A Scandal in Bohemia." (6—3 each)

19.  Rondo Hatton played the murderous Oxton Creeper. (2—1 each)

20. Whitehead was Holmes in *The Crucifer of Blood.* (3)

21. Lee played Sir Henry Baskerville in the 1959 Hammer Films' *Hound of the Baskervilles,* and he played Mycroft in *The Private Life of Sherlock Holmes.* (4—1 each)

22. *A Study in Terror* (3)

23. *The West End Horror* (1)

24. Sir Laurence Olivier (1)

25. *Sherlock Holmes in New York* (3)

26. Fritz Weaver was Holmes in the musical *Baker Street.* The actress is Inga Swenson, who is perhaps more familiar as Krause on the television series "Benson." (4—2 each; 2 for the bonus)

27. Douglas Wilmer (2)

28. Wilder appeared as Sigerson "Sigi" Holmes. (1)

29. Robert Stephens was Holmes and Colin Blakely was Watson. (2)

30. *Murder by Decree* (2)

31. William Shatner was the villainous Stapleton. (1)

32.     David Burke (2)

33.     Eric Porter (3)

34.     Charles Marowitz (1)

# Chapter 17
# The Final Problems

1.  What did Holmes squirt on the wheels of Dr. Armstrong's carriage to give the draghound Pompey a scent to follow?

2.  Twins are mentioned in only two of Holmes's many cases. Which two adventures brought him into contact with at least one half of an identical twosome?

3.  What color was the light on the clipper *Aurora*?

4.  What was the name of the murderer who approached Sherlock in '87 with the request that Holmes get him off?

5.  Where was Jefferson Hope employed when he made the pills which would

decide life or death for Drebber, Stangerson and himself?

6. Holmes once stated to Watson that when a member of this profession "goes wrong, he is the first of criminals." Which occupation did Holmes apprehend as a potential breeding ground for malefactors?

7. What did Hugo Oberstein use in corresponding with Colonel Valentine Walter in the agony column of the *Daily Telegraph*?

8. What was the name of the man who supplied Professor Presbury with his special serum which the Professor was using in an attempt to regain his youth?

9. How much older than Sherlock is Mycroft?

10. What was the one-word message Watson was to send Holmes if Josiah Amberley should somehow give the good doctor the slip?

11. What was the name of the girl mentioned in the note composed by Alec Cunningham and his father?

12. In "Adventure of the Engineer's Thumb" Holmes produced a newspaper clipping

which dealt with the disappearance of another engineer about a year earlier. What was the name of the murderous Ferguson's first victim?

13. What was the name of Jonas Oldacre's tailor? Hint: it was also the name—sans the final s—of one of the victims of the Scowrers.

14. Thaddeus Sholto sent Mary Morstan a note instructing her to be outside of which London theater?

15. In which church were Irene Adler and Godfrey Norton of the Inner Temple married?

16. Holmes could often tell a great deal about an individual just by examining an item owned by that person. What two clients inadvertently left possessions of theirs in Baker Street which the Master examined prior to making their actual acquaintance?

17. There was a date chiseled over "the low, heavy-lintelled door in the old part" of Hurlstone, the ancestral home of the Musgraves. What was it?

18. What were the three clubs to which Ronald Adair belonged, and at which of them had he played cards with Colonel Sebastian Moran?

19. Can you recall the name to which Jonas Oldacre had made out several large checks just prior to the Norwood builder's disappearance?

20. What was the name of Violet Smith's— the Solitary Cyclist of Charlington— fiancé?

21. In America Black Gorgiano had pressured Gennaro Lucca to murder his boss. What was the intended victim's name?

22. Holmes asked what Watson knew about two different diseases in "The Dying Detective." On what illnesses did the Master quiz his physician friend?

23. Henry Peters was traveling with a female accomplice. Can you recall the name of this *femme fatale*? Hint: It was also Lady Brackenstall's maiden name.

24. What was the name of the establishment which made the special coffin in which Lady Frances Carfax was concealed?

25. Holmes told Watson that Baron Adelbert Gruner had murdered his wife. Where did the Master claim the Baron had done in the Baroness?

26. Watson once posed as Dr. Hill Barton, an expert on Chinese pottery. What was the

fictitious address on the duplicitous doctor's calling card?

27. Holmes listed a number of atrocities committed by Count Sylvius; however, only
two victims were mentioned by name.
Can you remember either of the Count's
victims?

28. Name the firm responsible for bringing
"The Adventure of the Sussex Vampire"
to the attention of Sherlock.

29. Rodger Prescott, "Killer" Evans's partner,
had lived in Nathan Garrideb's rooms six
years previously. Under what name had
Prescott rented the rooms?

30. What was the name of the Master's
"general utility man who looked up
routine business"? Hint: Holmes consulted him in "The Adventure of the
Creeping Man."

31. According to Constable John Rance, what
was the drunk he helped in *A Study in
Scarlet* singing about?

32. A young man disguised as a woman
visited Holmes in *A Study in Scarlet*. He
did this in order to reclaim the ring which
Jefferson Hope had lost. What name did
he use in his meeting with Holmes?

33. What three qualities did Holmes tell Watson that the ideal detective must possess?

34. Sir Henry Baskerville received a warning letter composed of words cut from the *Times*. What was the only word in the letter not cropped from the paper?

35. As long as we are talking about hounds, can you recall the name of the family that would inherit everything should Sir Henry fall victim to the hound?

36. Who made the missing boot that Stapleton stole from Sir Henry so that the hound would have the baronet's scent?

37. What make bicycle was found in the bushes outside of John Douglas's home?

38. With regard to the same case, the local inspector, White Mason, used one word repeatedly to describe the events that were transpiring. What was the term which Mason used over and over?

39. McMurdo sang two songs to Ettie Shafter, his future wife. Can you remember either of them?

40. What name did McMurdo tell the members of the lodge that Birdy Edwards was using as an alias in *The Valley of Fear*?

41. In *The Valley of Fear,* can you recall the name of the county delegate who was even more powerful than McGinty—and probably more evil as well?

42. What were the names of the two killers who lodged with McMurdo and Scanlon just before they added to the number of murders they had committed?

43. What did the stablehand at King's Pyland have for dinner the night Silver Blaze disappeared?

44. Can you recall the name of Jonas Oldacre's housekeeper and confidante?

45. Two busts of Napoleon were purchased by a physician who obviously had a soft spot for the Little Corporal. What was the doctor's name?

46. Who was the constable covering the Holland Grove beat on the night that Enoch Drebber's body was found?

47. What is the name of the tavern in Nine Elms Lane?

48. What type of cartridges did Sherlock use in his revolver?

49. Can you recall the house-agents in Edgware Road from whom Nathan Garrideb leased his rooms?

50.  Finally, Holmes remembered it—can you?
     What was the *full* title of the King of
     Bohemia?